OKLAHOMA

DAILY DEVOTIONS FOR DIE-HARD FANS

SOONERS

OKLAHOMA

SOONERS

Daily Devotions for Die-Hard Fans

ACC
Clemson Tigers
Duke Blue Devils
FSU Seminoles
Georgia Tech Yellow Jackets
North Carolina Tar Heels
NC State Wolfpack
Virginia Cavaliers
Virginia Tech Hokies

BIG 10
Michigan Wolverines
Ohio State Buckeyes

BIG 12
Oklahoma Sooners
Oklahoma State Cowboys
TCU Horned Frogs
Texas Longhorns
Texas Tech Red Raiders

SEC
Alabama Crimson Tide
Arkansas Razorbacks
Auburn Tigers
More Auburn Tigers
Florida Gators
Georgia Bulldogs
Kentucky Wildcats
LSU Tigers
More Georgia Bulldogs
Mississippi State Bulldogs
Ole Miss Rebels
South Carolina Gamecocks
More South Carolina Gamecocks
Texas A&M Aggies
Tennessee Volunteers

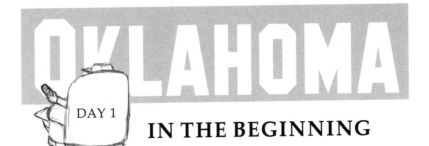

IN THE BEGINNING

Read Genesis 1, 2:1-3.

"God saw all that he had made, and it was very good" (v. 1:31).

When a few students brought out an old Spalding football on a fall afternoon in 1895, they really didn't know what to do with it. Jack Harts did, though, and he enthusiastically set about organizing the University of Oklahoma's first football team.

John A. Harts had played some football growing up in Kansas. While the first game in the Oklahoma Territory had taken place the year before, few of the 148 university students had ever even seen an organized contest. Nevertheless, the sight of that football inspired Harts. "Let's get up a football team!" he declared from a seat in the local barber shop.

Harts wasn't just empty bravado as he proceeded to assemble a team, coach it, captain it, and schedule a game. That first contest was played on Nov. 7, 1895, on a field of prairie grass north of the lone university building. Team members Joe Merkle and Jap Clapam provided the horses that pulled wagons of dirt to fill in the field's buffalo wallows.

The day before the game, Harts discovered that he was two players short of a full team, partly because he had suffered a knee injury in practice and couldn't play. He recruited the local barber, Bud Risinger, and Fred Perry, a 26-year old married man who drove Norman's street sprinkling wagon. No one seemed to mind that neither man was enrolled in the university.

From Oklahoma City, the opponent was a collection of high school and college students "and a couple of town toughs." They had already played some and it showed; they won easily 34-0.

OU's first football players disconsolately "trudged back to [the] barber shop where they washed up, dressed their wounds, and discussed the merits and demerits of football." Clapam declared that when he went home, he "was too sore to do the chores, but I sure slept good" that night.

Football at the University of Oklahoma had begun.

Beginnings are important, but what we make of them is even more important. Consider, for example, how far the OU football program has come since that beginning in 1895.

Every morning, as an expression of divine love, God hands to you a chance for a new beginning in the form of a new day full of promise and the chance to right the wrongs in your life. You can use the day to pay a debt, start a new relationship, tell your family you love them, replace a burned-out light bulb, chase a dream, solve a nagging problem . . . or not.

God simply provides the gift. How you use it is up to you. People often talk wistfully about starting over or making a new beginning. God gives you the chance with the dawning of every new day. You have the chance today to make things right – and that includes your relationship with God.

Football is all the rage at the university.
-- *The* Norman Transcript, *Nov. 30, 1894*

**Every day is not just a dawn
but a precious chance to start over or begin anew.**

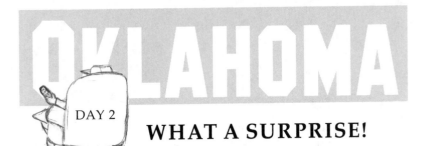

DAY 2

WHAT A SURPRISE!

Read 1 Thessalonians 5:1-11.

"But you, brothers, are not in darkness so that this day should surprise you like a thief" (v. 4).

Much of the known world may have been surprised by what the Sooners did in the 2001 Orange Bowl, but head coach Bob Stoops and his wife, Carol, sure weren't.

The game of Jan. 3 was merely a formality, a rite necessary to get on with the business of crowning the Florida State Seminoles the repeat national champions. The experts apparently believed that; they installed the Noles as 11-point favorites. "Florida State didn't give us the respect we deserved," groused All-American linebacker Rocky Calmus. But why should the FSU players be any different from anyone else? As Stoops pointed out before the game, "If the oddsmakers decided who won, we'd be 7-4."

But the Soooners weren't; They were 12-0 and Big-12 champs. "I think they probably questioned us because we had struggled against Oklahoma State [12-7] and then beat K-State by three points [27-24] in the Big 12 championship game," explained Josh Heupel, OU's first consensus All-American quarterback. In other words, said the pundits, the Seminoles were too good and the Sooners weren't good enough.

But as Stoops interrupted a reporter to say, "Hey, we have some athletes, too, you know." Those athletes had the benefit of "an audacious, ingenious defensive game plan that utterly befud-

SOONERS

dled" FSU's Heisman-Trophy winning quarterback. The offense that went into the Orange Bowl averaging 42.4 points a game didn't score a single point. FSU managed one measly safety in its 13-2 defeat as the Sooners grabbed their seventh national title.

Stoops and his wife weren't surprised one bit. After all, the morning of the game they shared an embrace and she said to him, "We're going to win. I know it." Hubby replied, "I know it too."

Surprise birthday parties are a delight. And what's the fun of opening Christmas presents when we already know what's in them? Some surprises in life -- such as winning the national title -- provide us with experiences that are both joyful and delightful.

Generally, though, we expend energy and resources to avoid most surprises and the impact they may have upon our lives. We may be surprised by the exact timing of a baby's arrival, but we nevertheless have the bags packed beforehand and the nursery all set for its occupant. Paul used this very image (v. 3) to describe the Day of the Lord, when Jesus will return to claim his own and establish his kingdom. We may be caught by surprise, but we must still be ready.

The consequences of being caught unprepared by a baby's insistence on being born are serious indeed. They pale, however, beside the eternal effects of not being ready when Jesus returns. We prepare ourselves just as Paul told us to (v. 8): We live in faith, hope, and love, ever on the alert for that great, promised day.

The result surprised [Bob] Stoops less than anyone else on earth.
-- Writer Austin Murphy on the 2001 Orange Bowl

The timing of Jesus' return will be a surprise;
the consequences should not be.

UNEXPECTEDLY

Read Matthew 24:36-51.

"No one knows about that day or hour, not even the angels in heaven, nor the Son, but only the Father" (v. 36).

Something totally unexpected happened to Patty Gasso one day during a softball game: She gave her life to Christ.

SoonerSports.com unabashedly declares that Gasso is the best coach in the history of OU softball. That same site further asserts Gasso to be the greatest coach in Big 12 history. Few would argue.

During the 2012 season, her 18th as OU's head coach, Gasso won the 1,000th game of her storied career. She has won more games than any other coach in Big 12 history. Since she took the Sooner program over before the 1995 season, every single one of her teams has made it to postseason play; her OU squads have never failed to win at least forty games in a season. The Sooners won the national title in 2000 and in 2013.

As much as anything else, boredom brought Gasso to Norman. She was the head coach at Long Beach Community College, a California junior college, and was looking for a new challenge. She went to the College World Series in 1994 with no particular aim in mind, but while she was there, she wound up talking to an associate athletics director from OU. The conversation turned into an interview that turned into a job offer. So she packed up and headed east.

Gasso was already accustomed to God's using softball to do

unexpected things in her life. In 1986, she married Jim Gasso, a Christian who had grown up in the Church. Persistent witness from her husband and an assistant coach convicted Gasso that something was indeed missing in her life.

Thus, in 1992, during a game, while she was coaching from the third-base box, Gasso surrendered her life to Christ. "It was so joyful," she said about the unexpected experience. "It ran through me. It felt like I was able to exhale and move forward."

We usually live our daily lives convinced that we've got everything figured out and under control, and then something unexpected happens to let us know how wrong we are. About the only thing we can expect from life with any certainty is the unexpected.

God is that way too, suddenly showing up to remind us he's still around -- even if it's during a college softball game. A friend calls and tells you he's praying for you, a child or grandchild hugs you, a lone lily blooms in your yard -- unexpected moments when the divine comes crashing into our lives with such clarity that it takes our breath away and brings tears to our eyes.

But why shouldn't God do the unexpected? The only factor limiting what God can do in our lives is the paucity of our own faith. We should expect the unexpected from God, this same deity who caught everyone by surprise by unexpectedly coming to live among us as a man, and who will return when we least expect it.

It was undeniably what it was supposed to feel like.
-- Patty Gasso on unexpectedly giving her life to Christ

God continually does the unexpected,
like showing up as Jesus,
who will return unexpectedly.

REVELATION

Read Isaiah 53.

"But he was pierced for our transgressions, he was crushed for our iniquities; the punishment that brought us peace was upon him, and by his wounds we are healed"
(v. 5).

Barry Switzer called it "one of the greatest things I ever saw or participated in." It was the 1977 game between Ohio State and Oklahoma, and one Sooner player knew exactly how it would end.

The game at Columbus on Sept. 24 was the first time the two traditional powerhouses had ever played each other. The Buckeyes led 28-26 with 1:29 left when defensive back Mike Babb recovered an onside kick. Dean Blevins then hit end Steve Rhodes with a pass to the OSU 32 and kept on the option to the 23. With only six seconds left, Uwe von Schamann trotted onto the field.

The first time he saw football, von Schamann, a native of Germany, thought it was "a silly, stupid game. It looked like a bunch of guys with crash helmets on," he said. One day in a high-school PE class, however, he picked up a ball and kicked it. A coach saw it and on the spot asked him to come out for football.

The coaches instructed him on the difference between kicking a soccer ball and a football, and von Schamann caught on quickly. He caught on so well, in fact, that after his junior season, a coach told him he could land a scholarship. "What's a scholarship?" von Schamann asked.

SOONERS

That scholarship brought him to Norman and "one of the defining moments of Oklahoma football history." He was so calm and so confident that night against Ohio State that as the crowd chanted "Block that kick!" he actually led them like a conductor. Then he booted a 41-yard field goal for the 29-28 win.

Exactly as his roommate and holder Bud Hebert had predicted. Before the game, Hebert told von Schamann he had dreamed the junior kicker would win the game with a field goal.

In our jaded age, we have pretty much relegated prophecy to dark rooms in which mysterious women peer into crystal balls or clasp our sweaty palms while uttering some vague generalities. At best, we understand a prophet as someone who predicts future events as Bud Hebert did.

Within the pages of the Bible, though, we encounter something radically different. A prophet is a messenger from God, one who relays divine revelation to others.

Prophets seem somewhat foreign to us because in one very real sense the age of prophecy is over. In the name of Jesus, we have access to God through our prayers and through scripture. In searching for God's will for our lives, we seek divine revelation. We may speak only for ourselves and not for the greater body of Christ, but we do not need a prophet to discern what God would have us do. We need faith in the one whose birth, life, and death fulfilled more than 300 Bible prophecies.

Hey, the dream's gonna come true.
-- Uwe von Schamann to Bud Hebert before 'The Kick'

**Persons of faith continuously seek a word
from God for their lives.**

REVELATION   9

DAY 5

GIFT-WRAPPED

Read James 1:13-18.

"Every good and perfect gift is from above, coming down from the Father of the heavenly lights" (v. 17).

Jason White got quite a birthday present: quarterbacks coach Chuck Long told him he was the team's starter.

For four seasons in Norman, not too much went right for White. As a freshman in 1999, he hurt his back in the weight room and received a medical redshirt. During the national championship season of 2000, he was so far down the depth chart that he finally convinced the coaches to let him quarterback the scout team.

Junior Nate Hybl won the starting job for 2001, but he was injured early in the Texas game and White went in. OU beat the 5th-ranked Horns 14-3, and White was the starter two weeks later. In the Nebraska game the next week, though, he tore his ACL and was out for the rest of the season.

White earned the starting job over Hybl in 2002 despite misgivings about his knee. In the second game, he tore the ACL of his other knee. The first thing that came into his mind was, "Why? Why? Am I supposed to be playing football?"

In the spring of 2003, he decided he wasn't. His knee was still hurting him, so he told Long he was done with football. "Don't give up," Long encouraged him. "Keep trying."

White stayed with it. And then on June 19th, his 23rd birthday, he was doing passing drills when Long gave him an unexpected,

SOONERS

shocking gift. The coach told him, "Coach [Bob] Stoops wants to name you the starter right now."

The rest, of course, is Sooner legend. White led the team into the BCS National Championship Game that season and became the first OU quarterback in history to win the Heisman Trophy.

"Every night of that season as we won one game and then the next," White said, "I thought about how glad I was that I had stayed." And that he had received that birthday gift.

Receiving a gift is nice, but giving has its pleasures too, doesn't it? The children's excitement on Christmas morning. That smile of pure delight on your spouse's face when you came up with a really cool anniversary present. Your dad's surprise that time you didn't give him a tie or socks. There really does seem to be something to this being more blessed to give than to receive.

No matter how generous we may be, though, we are grumbling misers compared to God, who is the greatest gift-giver of all. That's because all the good things in our lives – every one of them – come from God. Friends, love, health, family, the air we breathe, the sun that warms us, even our very lives are all gifts from a profligate God. And here's the kicker: He even gives us eternal life with him through the gift of his son.

What in the world can we possibly give God in return? Our love and our life.

From what we get, we can make a living; what we give makes a life.
– Arthur Ashe

Nobody can match God when it comes to giving,
but you can give him the gift
of your love in appreciation.

TEACHER'S PET

Read John 3:1-15.

"[Nicodemus] came to Jesus at night and said, 'Rabbi, we know you are a teacher who has come from God'" (v. 2).

How can a coach win who wore a suit on the sideline, didn't have any training rules, and ran short, light practices? In Bud Wilkinson's case, he won in large part because he was a teacher.

From 1947-1963, Wilkinson won 145 games and three national titles as OU's head football coach, but he never fit the stereotype of the coach. He was soft-spoken; he was a meticulous dresser who usually wore a gray flannel suit on the sideline for games; he didn't believe in training rules; his teams never scrimmaged once the season started; his practices were generally light workouts.

Writer Booton Herndon said Wilkinson won "with such intangibles as philosophical attitudes, inner faith and conviction, and unswerving moral determination." Just like football, he taught those, and in teaching lay the secret of the coach's success.

As a sophomore in 1954, Jerry Tubbs was the third-string center. He had never carried the ball in his life, but Wilkinson nevertheless moved him to fullback only a few days before the TCU game. Tubbs quickly caught on to the new position except for the open-field block on the defensive end.

So Wilkinson, who disliked being dirty so much that he wore different shoes if the sideline were muddy for a game, got right down in the wet grass and the mud that day to show Tubbs how to execute that block. "I found it kind of embarrassing," Tubbs said. "You know how personally clean he is."

Wilkinson didn't just do it once. He threw the block repeatedly, "getting down in the mud and picking himself up out of it, until I guess I just felt miserable," Tubbs said. "Here was this man, the country's leading coach, trying to show me how to do something."

Against TCU, Tubbs executed his blocks. Two seasons later, he was All-America. He was taught well.

You can read this book, break 90 on the golf course, and do your job because somebody taught you. And as you learn, you become the teacher yourself. You teach your children how to play Monopoly and how to drive a car. You show rookies the ropes at the office and teach baseball's basics to a Little League team.

This pattern of learning and then teaching includes your spiritual life also. Somebody taught you about Jesus, and this, too, you must pass on. Jesus came to teach a truth the religious teachers and the powerful of his day did not want to hear. Little has changed in that regard, as the world today often reacts with scorn and disdain to Jesus' message.

Nothing, not even death itself, could stop Jesus from teaching his lesson of life and salvation. So should nothing stop you from teaching life's most important lesson: Jesus saves.

[Bud Wilkinson] believes he can teach more football conversationally than he can by having his men knock their heads together.
-- Writer Booton Herndon on why OU didn't scrimmage

In life, you learn and then you teach,
which includes learning and teaching about Jesus,
the most important lesson of all.

DAY 7

WORK ETHIC

Read Matthew 9:35-38.

"Then he said to his disciples, 'The harvest is plentiful but the workers are few. Ask the Lord of the harvest, therefore, to send out workers into his harvest field'" (vv. 37-38).

Blake Griffin knew exactly where he got his willingness to work hard from: his upbringing and his faith in Christ.

Griffin was both the national player of the year and the Big 12 Player of the Year in 2009 as a sophomore. He led the nation in rebounding and double doubles and was second in field-goal percentage. His 504 rebounds were both a school and a league single-season record. He joined Wayman Tisdale and Alvan Adams as the only Sooners in history to score at least 1,000 points in their first two seasons.

Griffin was expected to be a lottery pick after he led OU in 2007-08 to a 23-12 record and the second round of the NCAA Tournament as a freshman, but he decided to return. The team went 30-6 and advanced to the Elite 8. During that storied season, Griffin averaged 22.7 points and 14.4 rebounds per game.

Griffin had good reasons for waiting a year to turn pro: He wanted to play one more season with his older brother, Taylor, and he knew he had work to do to become a better player. And therein lay the key to Griffin's success. While he had the God-given size (6-10 and 251 lbs.), he also had a work ethic that drove him to excel. His parents and his faith were behind that.

SOONERS

Griffin was home-schooled until the seventh grade and was then coached at Oklahoma Christian School by his father. The Griffin boys had "two strong Christian role models to constantly look up to and emulate." That emulation meant hard work.

"It's made such a difference," Blake declared about his Christian upbringing. On the court, it means he plays all out and doesn't "hold anything back," he said. "That's just kind of the way we were brought up -- to not leave anything behind."

In other words, to work hard -- and the result was a storied OU career and 53 Sooner wins in two seasons.

Do you embrace hard work or try to avoid it? No matter how hard you may try, you really can't escape hard work. Funny thing about all these labor-saving devices like cell phones and laptop computers: You're working longer and harder than ever. For many of us, our work defines us perhaps more than any other aspect of our lives. But there's a workforce you're a part of that doesn't show up in any Labor Department statistics or any IRS records.

You're part of God's staff; God has a specific job that only you can do for him. It's often referred to as a "calling," but it amounts to your serving God where there is a need in the way that best suits your God-given abilities and talents

You should stand ready to work for God all the time, 24-7. Those are awful hours, but the benefits are out of this world.

That's one of the things I ask God for, to help me play the game the way it's supposed to be played.
— Blake Griffin on playing hard

God calls you to work for him; whether you're a worker or a malingerer is up to you.

A CHANGE OF PLANS

Read Genesis 18:20-33.

"The Lord said, 'If I find fifty righteous people in the city of Sodom, I will spare the whole place for their sake'" (v. 26).

The national championship and the 30th straight win were slipping away -- until a change of plans at halftime.

Bud Wilkinson's 1955 Sooners made their debut in Chapel Hill, NC, under conditions so humid that trainer Ken Rawlinson said, "Although the sun was shining brightly, it was raining." It didn't matter; neither the weather nor the opposing football teams could stop OU that fall.

"We wanted to beat everybody 40-zip," said halfback Clendon Thomas, an All-America as a senior in 1957 who was inducted into the College Football Hall of Fame in 2011. The Sooners dominated their foes. They led the nation in total offense by a wide margin, rolling up 410.7 yards per game. Senior guard Bo Bolinger and junior halfback Tommy McDonald were All-Americas.

All that star power and domination didn't impress the Maryland Terrapins one bit, however. They arrived in Miami for the Orange Bowl confident they could whip Oklahoma and win the national title themselves. They were good. UCLA's head coach had tabbed them "the greatest team of the era." Moreover, they were coached by Jim Tatum, who had led the Sooners in 1946.

The Terrapins were indeed ready. They led 6-0 at halftime; the

SOONERS

Sooners were in deep trouble. So an unhappy Wilkinson changed the game plan. He ordered quarterback Jimmy Harris to run the "go-go" offense. It was a no-huddle attack with Harris calling the plays at the line of scrimmage.

The Terrapins never stood a chance. "We were running plays while Maryland was still getting up off the ground," McDonald recalled. The Terps soon faltered under the relentless pressure.

Thanks to that change in plans, OU won 20-6.

To be unable to adapt to changing circumstances to is stultify and die. It's true of animal life, of business and industry, of the military, of sports teams, of you and your relationships, your job, and your finances.

Changing your plans regularly therefore is rather routine for you. But consider how remarkable it is that the God of the universe may change his mind about something. What could bring that about?

Prayer. Someone -- an old nomad named Abraham or a 21st-century Sooner fan like you -- talks to God, who listens and considers what is asked of him.

You may feel uncomfortable praying. Maybe you're reluctant and embarrassed; perhaps you feel you're not very good at it. But nobody majors in prayer at school, and as for being reluctant, what have you got to lose? Your answer may even be a change of plans on God's part. Such is the power of prayer.

Get out of the way! Here they come again!
-- Maryland lineman John Sandusky in the last half to a teammate

**Prayer is so powerful that it may even
change God's mind.**

PRESSURE POINT

Read 1 Kings 18:16-40.

"Answer me, O Lord, answer me, so these people will know that you, O Lord, are God" (v. 37).

The place was "a cauldron of noise and pressure," and the Sooners were in real trouble. So all they did was ignore the pressure and pull out a big-time win.

On Sept. 17, 2011, the Sooners traveled to Tallahassee, Fla., for an early intersectional showdown with the Seminoles of FSU. The Tallahassee folks viewed this game as a crucial step on the Noles' return to football prominence.

And they played like it. When FSU tied the game at 13-13 with less than ten minutes left to play, "Doak [Campbell Stadium] was deafening. Doubt was creeping into the minds of Sooners fans, who had seen this movie before." That is, the Sooners had shown a distressing tendency of late not to respond well to the pressure of playing on the road.

This was one of those times when the pressure on the road was pretty intense. FSU had all the momentum, the crowd was out of its collective mind, and the Sooners hadn't taken a single second-half snap in Seminole territory. The situation didn't improve with the kickoff, which backed the offense up to its own 17.

So quarterback Landry Jones and his teammates proceeded to put on "a steely display of poise, power and playmaking." They calmly and methodically covered that 83 yards with Jones hitting

5 of 6 passes for 73 of them. The last 37 came on a touchdown toss to sophomore wide receiver Kenny Stills.

They weren't through. The defense hauled in an interception, and the offense "muscled up and pounded out" seven straight runs from Dominique Whaley. Those 32 yards of smashmouth football ate up clock and yielded a game-clinching field goal.

OU won 23-13, demonstrating what head coach Bob Stoops called the best character showing in the fourth quarter since 2000.

You live every day with pressure. As Elijah did so long ago, you lay it on the line with everybody watching. Your family, co-workers, or employees – they depend on you. You know the pressure of a deadline, of a job evaluation, of taking the risk of asking someone to go out with you, of driving in rush-hour traffic.

Help in dealing with daily pressure is readily available, and the only price you pay for it is your willingness to believe. God will give you the grace to persevere if you ask prayerfully.

And while you may need some convincing, the pressures of daily living are really small potatoes since they all will pass. The real pressure comes when you stare into the face of eternity because what you do with it is irrevocable and forever. You can handle that pressure easily enough by deciding for Jesus. Eternity is then taken care of; the pressure's off – forever.

They sense blood, the stadium's on you, they have the momentum, and we just seized it right back.
    -- Bob Stoops on his team's response to the pressure vs. FSU

**The greatest pressure you face in life
concerns where you will spend eternity,
which can be dealt with by deciding for Jesus.**

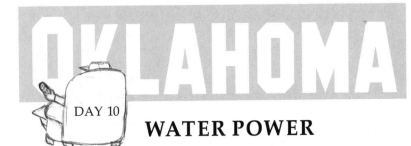

WATER POWER

Read Acts 10:34-48.

"Can anyone keep these people from being baptized with water? They have received the Holy Spirit just as we have" (v. 47).

Jim Tatum was so intense that during his first game at OU, he took a drink out of -- well, it was a less than sanitary container.

Tatum spent one season -- 1946 -- as the Sooners' head football coach. His first game was at Army, and he wanted his team to look as good as the opposition. Quarterback Jack Mitchell recalled that all OU had was old leather helmets while "everybody knew that Army wore those modern Riddell helmets." Tatum decided his team had to have those modern, spiffy headpieces, too.

One day at practice, Tatum was missing until a big truck drove onto the practice field. "Guess who is sitting on top of the truck?" Mitchell asked. "That's right, Tatum." In that truck was a load of Riddell helmets that Tatum proceeded to toss onto the ground.

The game marked the first time the Sooners had ever traveled by plane. To add to Tatum's anxiety, the game was generally regarded in Norman as the most important one in Oklahoma history, considering the opponent, the new coach, the influx of new talent, and President Harry Truman's presence. "Come game time, Tatum was so nervous, he was taping ankles just to keep focused," Mitchell said.

Tatum's intensity only increased as the game wore on. He never did settle down, cussing and fretting and complaining to the refs. "He got all excited on the sideline," summarized All-American tackle Buddy Burris. Then at one point during the game, Tatum did something Burris could not believe.

The intense head coach wanted some water but didn't have any nearby. "So one of the guys was [on the bench]," Burris said, "soaking his feet in water. Jim went over and picked up the bucket and drank it. I thought he had just about lost his marbles."

He had, though, found some water.

Children's wading pools and swimming pools in the backyard. Fishing, boating, skiing, and swimming at a lake. Sun, sand, and surf at the beach. If there's any water around, we'll probably be in it, on it, or near it. If there's not any at hand, we'll build a dam and create our own.

We love the wet stuff for its recreational uses, but water first and foremost is about its absolute necessity to support and maintain life. From its earliest days, the Christian church appropriated water as an image of life through the ritual of baptism.

Since the time of the arrival of the Holy Spirit at Pentecost, baptism with water has been the symbol of entry into the Christian community. It is water that marks a person as belonging to Jesus. It is through water that a person proclaims that Jesus is his Lord.

There's something in the water, all right. There is life.

Swimmers are like tea bags; you don't know how strong they are until you put them in the water.

— *Source unknown*

**There is life in the water:
physical life and spiritual life.**

GOD'S CONQUERORS

Read John 16:19-33.

*"In this world you will have trouble. But take heart! I
have overcome the world" (v. 33b).*

All football players overcome obstacles to make it as a starter
at the college level. No one else in OU history, however, has overcome what Jeff Resler did: He didn't have a left hand.

Resler started at right guard in 1991 as a redshirt freshman. He
was the first OU freshman to become a full-time starter on the
offensive line since Anthony Phillips in 1985.

When Resler was born, his right big toe was shorter than usual,
and his right index and middle fingers were also shorter than
usual and were fused together. That was disconcerting enough,
but the worse was yet to come.

As Resler told it, "The umbilical cord was wrapped around my
wrist, and the circulation was cut off. It was just dead, so . . ." So
seven days after Resler was born, his left hand was amputated.

"I guess [God] just didn't make me all," Resler once said. Maybe
not, but God certainly gave Resler a hearty helping of an indomitable spirit that would not let a handicap even slow him down.

He played baseball until junior high school. He consistently
beat his dad in golf. He wrestled in high school and was the state
champion in the shot put. Using a prosthesis, he even did the
weightlifting that a lineman must do. "My parents never told me I
couldn't do anything," he said. Except perhaps for one thing: His

mom replaced all the cuff buttons on his shirts with snaps.

"It's amazing what he does," said Merv Johnson, OU's offensive line coach, about his starting guard. "If you could get every kid on your squad to max out like Jeff has, just think what you could accomplish."

"You just have to use your body more and just give all you have," Resler said about battling his two-handed opponents. In the opening game of the '91 season, he noticed the player across the line gave him a funny look on the first play. OU won 40-2.

We often hear inspiring stories of people like Jeff Resler who triumph over especially daunting obstacles. Those barriers may be physical or mental disabilities or great personal tragedies or injustice. When we hear of them, we may well respond with a little prayer of thanksgiving that life has been kinder to us.

But all people of faith, no matter how drastic the obstacles they face, must ultimately overcome the same opponent: the Satan-infested world. Some do have it tougher than others, but we all must fight daily to remain confident and optimistic.

To merely survive from day to day is to give up by surrendering our trust in God's involvement in our daily life. To overcome, however, is to stand up to the world and fight its temptations that would erode the armor of our faith in Jesus Christ.

Today is a day for you to overcome by remaining faithful. The very hosts of Heaven wait to hail the conquering hero.

It never occurred to me that I couldn't.
-- Jeff Resler on playing football for Oklahoma

Life's difficulties provide us a chance to
experience the true joy of victory in Jesus.

TOUGH COOKIES

Read 2 Corinthians 11:21b-29.

"Besides everything else, I face daily the pressure of my concern for all the churches" (v. 28).

When OU fans reminisce about the 2011-12 women's basketball team, they will almost certainly focus on one quality: This was one tough bunch. They had to be.

In a program that has fielded some legendary teams, this particular squad wasn't projected to be among the greatest. They were pre-season picks to finish fourth in the Big 12, and that was before the season devolved into one session after another in which head coach Sherri Coale delivered bad news to her team.

Senior guard Jasmine Hartman tore her knee up and ended her season before it even started. Junior center Lyndsey Cloman pretty much did the same, her knee injury coming in a preseason exhibition game.

Coale had to call her team together in November to deliver the awful news that two Oklahoma State coaches they all knew had been killed in a plane crash. Then right before the Kansas State game of Jan. 17, Coale was at it again, informing her team that starting forward Joanna McFarland, the team's leading rebounder, had suffered a broken jaw and was out indefinitely.

So the season went. Circumstances forced Coale to change the lineup constantly and rely on youngsters whom she had expected to spend the season learning about play in the Big 12.

SOONERS

So what happened? Coale called on her team to be tough, and they responded. "We just stressed the fact that tough teams aren't affected by difficulties," the head coach said. And so the Sooners just kept fighting.

Defying the low expectations and the odds, they won 21 games, finished second in the conference, and beat Michigan by 21 points in the first round of the NCAA Tournament. Tough enough.

You don't have to be an OU basketball player to be tough. In America today, toughness isn't restricted to physical accomplishments and brute strength. Going to work every morning even when you feel bad, sticking by your rules for your children in a society that ridicules parental authority, making hard decisions about your aging parents' care often over their objections — you've got to be tough every day just to live honorably, decently, and justly.

Living faithfully requires toughness, too, though in America chances are pretty good that you won't be imprisoned, stoned, or flogged this week for your faith as Paul was. Still, contemporary society exerts subtle, psychological, daily pressures on you to turn your back on your faith and your values. Popular culture promotes promiscuity, atheism, and gutter language; your children's schools have kicked God out; the corporate culture advocates amorality before the shrine of the almighty dollar.

You have to hang tough to keep the faith.

Tough teams find a way to win. We've done that for the most part.
— Sherri Coale on the team of 2011-12

Life demands more than mere physical toughness;
you must be spiritually tough too.

HOMEBODIES

Read 2 Corinthians 5:1-10.

"We . . . would prefer to be away from the body and at home with the Lord" (v. 8).

Rick Bryan was so homesick that he spent his first two days in Norman crying and praying.

Bryan missed out on a lot of football growing up because of a back injury he suffered in the seventh grade. Not until his sophomore year in high school did his parents agree to let him play football again. "I was scared to death," he said about suiting up again. "I hadn't played in three years and now I was playing against guys two or three years older than me."

But Bryan was big enough and good enough to become an immediate starter both ways. Still, as his high-school career wore on, he never considered playing at OU. "I figured I would never be good enough to play for the great Oklahoma Sooners," he said. But he was.

So Bryan left home in August 1980, and it was not a pleasant experience for him. "I was lost," he admitted. "I wasn't even five miles from my house when I became homesick. I didn't want to leave." On the drive, Bryan said, "I started talking to God and I know He listened to me the entire way there."

When he arrived, Bryan discovered to his dismay that he was two days early. He came to close to getting in his car and heading back home but realized that if he did, he wouldn't come back. So

SOONERS

this lonely, homesick freshman spent the next two days in his freshman dorm room with only a bunk bed, a desk, and a closet. He left the room only to eat, spending the two days lying in his bed, crying, talking to God, and crying some more.

He said later that he figured that after two days the Lord got tired of listening to him. "He finally told me, in my mind, to go out and do the best I could," Bryan said. "He would give me the strength to survive."

That's exactly what happened. That scared and homesick freshman went on to become a two-time All-American defensive lineman and the Big Eight Defensive Player of the Year in 1982.

Home is not necessarily a matter of geography. It may be that place you share with your spouse and your children, whether it's Oklahoma or Alaska. You may feel at home when you return to Norman wondering why you were so eager to leave in the first place. Maybe the home you grew up in still feels like an old shoe, a little worn but comfortable and inviting.

God planted that sense of home in us because he is a God of place, and our place is with him. Thus, we may live a few blocks away from our parents and grandparents or we may relocate every few years, but we will still sometimes feel as though we don't really belong no matter where we are. We don't; our true home is with God in the place Jesus has gone ahead to prepare for us. We are homebodies and we are perpetually homesick.

I was scared, I was homesick, and I was lost.
-- Rick Bryan on arriving in Norman

We are continually homesick for our real home, which is with God in Heaven.

GOOD SPORTS

Read Titus 2:1-8.

"Show integrity, seriousness and soundness of speech that cannot be condemned, so that those who oppose you may be ashamed because they have nothing bad to say about us" (vv. 7b, 8).

How in the world do you react to your first loss in more than four years? If you're Oklahoma, you show sportsmanship that's just as legendary as the defeat.

The Sooners suffered perhaps the most famous loss in college football history on Nov. 16, 1957, when Notre Dame upset them 7-0. The defeat ended the Sooners' 47-game win streak, still college football's all-time record. The shutout was the first for OU in 112 games, at the time a record also.

It wasn't just after the loss that OU's sportsmanship revealed itself. With 3:50 to play in the scoreless game, the Irish sat at the Sooner 3 with fourth and goal. The frenzied crowd was yelling so loudly that the Notre Dame players couldn't hear the signals. With one of the biggest plays in college football history on the line, several Oklahoma players stood and motioned the crowd to be quiet. The rabid OU fans obeyed them. Notre Dame scored.

When the game ended, PA announcer Bruce Drake urged the crowd to "give a warm ovation to that Notre Dame team for breaking the 47-game winning streak." Still milling about in disbelief, the crowd did. Then Drake said, "Now let's give the team that give us 47 straight great Saturdays some applause." A stadium full of heartbroken fans got to their feet, applauded, and cheered. "I always thought that was pretty classy," said Leon Cross, a future All-America and a freshman that year.

The following Monday at the weekly meeting of the Oklahoma City Quarterback Club, the three hundred fans were ready when head coach Bud Wilkinson got up to speak. They stood and slowly began counting in unison, all the way through forty-seven.

Even in defeat, the Sooners were big-time winners.

One of life's paradoxes is that many who would never consider cheating on the tennis court or the racquetball court to gain an advantage think nothing of doing so in other areas of their life. In other words, the good sportsmanship they practice on the golf course or even on the Monopoly board doesn't carry over. They play with the truth, cut corners, abuse others verbally and run roughshod over them, and generally cheat whenever they can to gain an advantage on the job or in their personal relationships.

But good sportsmanship is a way of living, not just of playing. Shouldn't you accept defeat without complaint (You don't have to like it.); win gracefully without gloating; treat your competition with fairness, courtesy, generosity, and respect? That's the way one team treats another in the name of sportsmanship. That's the way one person treats another in the name of Jesus.

They were strictly big league about it.
   -- Notre Dame coach Terry Brennan on OU"s reaction to the loss

**Sportsmanship -- treating others with courtesy,
fairness, and respect -- is a way of living,
not just a way of playing.**

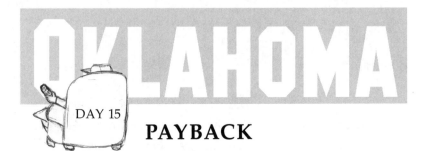

PAYBACK

Read Matthew 5:38-42.

*"I tell you, Do not resist an evil person. If someone strikes
you on the right cheek, turn to him the other also" (v. 39).*

There is payback and then there is what Oklahoma did to Texas
Tech.

In 2007, the Red Raiders upset Oklahoma 34-27, thus knocking
them out of the national title hunt. The Sooners did not forget.
Defensive coordinator Brent Venables started talking Texas Tech
before his charges even left the visitors' locker room after the 66-
28 beatdown of Texas A&M on Nov. 8, 2008.

Venables had no time to waste in getting his defense ready for
Tech's high-powered offense. "He told us everything that was
coming," said sophomore defensive tackle Gerald McCoy, a two-
time All-America. "Everything he said they would do, they did."

So the Sooners were more than prepared to hand out some
payback when Tech swaggered into Memorial Stadium on Nov.
22. On the other hand, "the Red Raiders were completely unprepared for the world of hurt awaiting them." They were ranked
No. 2; the once-beaten Sooners were sitting at No. 5. Oklahoma
mauled them 65-21.

The Sooners had 402 yards of offense by halftime and led 42-7.
OU sophomore quarterback Sam Bradford threw for 304 yards
and four touchdowns on only nineteen attempts. OU ran just as
easily as Bradford threw, amassing 299 yards on the ground. De-

SOONERS

Marco Murray ran for 125; Chris Brown added another 108.

The players insisted they didn't have revenge on their minds, but they clearly were out to do more than just beat Tech. "When you manhandle someone," Brown said, "you're basically taking their manhood."

Oklahoma took just about whatever it wanted from Tech.

The very nature of a rivalry such as OU and Texas Tech is that the loser will seek payback for the defeat of the season before. But what about in life when somebody's done you wrong; is it time to get even?

The problem with revenge in real-life is that it isn't as clear-cut as a scoreboard. Life is so messy that any attempt at revenge is often inadequate or, worse, backfires and injures you.

As a result, you remain gripped by your resentment and anger, which hurts you and no one else. You poison your own happiness while that other person goes blithely about her business. The only way someone who has hurt you can keep hurting you is if you're a willing participant.

But it doesn't have to be that way. Jesus ushered in a new way of living when he taught that we are not to seek revenge for personal wrongs and injuries. Let it go and go on with your life. What a relief!

Last year in Lubbock, they got after us. We vowed this time around to be the more physical team.
> -- *Running back Chris Brown on paying Tech back in 2008*

**Resentment and anger over a wrong injures you,
not the other person, so forget it --
just as Jesus taught.**

DAY 16

TEAM PLAYERS

Read 1 Corinthians 12:4-13, 27-31.

"Now to each one the manifestation of the Spirit is given for the common good" (v. 7).

We didn't have any superstars," declared Oklahoma's senior center fielder Chip Glass. So how, then, did the Sooners win the 1994 national title? Teamwork.

Oklahoma was good all season long, finishing the regular season at 42-17. In the long and storied history of OU baseball, though, that record doesn't particularly stand out. But as head coach Larry Cochell put it, "We got hot at the right time."

They did indeed. The Sooners got so hot they went undefeated in both the regional and the College World Series and trailed in only one of the 72 innings they played in the entire NCAA Tournament. They were untouchable in the regional in Austin, blasting Arkansas State 10-3 and Stanford 10-4 and beating Texas twice on its home field 15-4 and 6-3.

At Omaha, the Sooners became only the fifth team in NCAA history to sweep through the field undefeated. "The momentum that we got in Austin carried over," explained Cochell. The numbers tell the truth about how good a team the Sooners were in Omaha. They were the top hitting team (.327) and the top pitching team (2.37 ERA).

Glass led the way. The series' Most Outstanding Player, he hit three home runs after hitting three all season and batted .389.

After nipping Auburn 5-4 and topping Arizona State twice 4-3 and 6-1, the Sooners met Georgia Tech needing only one win to claim the title. They got it with another true team effort, winning easily 13-5; in the process they set a championship game record for runs and tied the all-time record with 16 hits.

"This was a team in the truest sense of the word," Glass said. "We all pulled together and did what it took to win."

Most accomplishments are the result of teamwork, whether it's a college baseball team, the running of a household, the completion of a project at work, or a dance recital. Disparate talents and gifts work together for the common good and the greater goal.

A church works exactly the same way. At its most basic, a church is a team that has been and is being assembled by God. A shared faith drives the team members and impels them toward shared goals. As a successful OU baseball team must have hitters, fielders, and pitchers, so must a church be composed of people with different spiritual and personal gifts. The result is something greater than everyone involved.

What makes a church team different from others is that the individual efforts are expended for the glory of God and not self. The nature of a church member's particular talents doesn't matter; what does matter is that those talents are used as part of God's team.

Twenty-five guys pulling on the same rope.
— Motto of the 1994 OU baseball team

**A church is a team of people using
their various talents and gifts for God,
the source of all those abilities to begin with.**

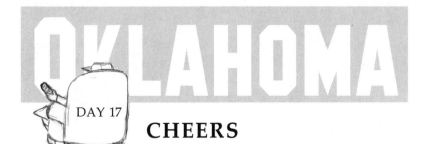

DAY 17

CHEERS

Read Matthew 21:1-11.

"The crowds that went ahead of him and those that followed shouted" (v. 9).

Humpty Dumpty, Whoop to do; What's the matter with Okla. U.?" So went a rousing cheer in the early days of OU football.

In the fall of 1898, pioneering head coach V.L. Parrington (See Devotion No. 86.) arranged a game for his new varsity team in Arkansas City. Fred and Joe, the Merkle brothers, led the Norman lads to a 5-0 win. After the game, the players encountered their first-ever custom-built bathtub and spent some time jumping into it two at a time to wash away the grime from the game.

When the triumphant players arrived home the next morning, a mournful sight greeted them. At the depot, "an old gentleman stood pensively next to his horse-drawn wagon which was filled with fresh straw." He was John Merkle, father of Fred and Joe, who had come to fetch the battered, broken bodies of his boys home. They were, of course, in rip-roaring shape and "rode home with their dad on the buckboard, smiling broadly."

Football was catching on, but the number one sport on the nascent campus at the turn of the century was the oratorical contest. At these gatherings, "noisy partisans from the four corners of the territory roused the crowds with clever yells." A number of cheers expressly for the football games soon arose, among them the "Humpty Dumpty" yell quoted above.

SOONERS

An Oklahoma Yell Card from 1910, urging the bearer to take it with him to the game, lists several yells, including "Rackity, Yackity, Yackity, Yack; Hullabaloo, Hullabaloo, How do you do." Yell number five on the card was apparently a group-wide "Giant Sneeze." Enthusiastic fans also took part in "15 rahs." Then there was the ever popular "Hi! Rickety! Hoop-te-do! Boomer! Sooner! Oklahoma U!" Enthusiasm ran high for the early OU football teams, known as of 1898 as the Rough Riders.

Chances are you go to work every day, do your job well, and then go home to your family. This country couldn't run without you; you're indispensable to the nation's efficiency. Even so, nobody cheers for you or waves pompoms in your face. Your name probably will never elicit a standing ovation when a PA announcer calls it.

It's just as well, since public opinion is notoriously fickle. Consider what happened to Jesus. When he entered Jerusalem, he was the object of raucous cheering and an impromptu parade. The crowd's adulation reached such a frenzy they tore branches off trees and threw their clothes on the ground.

Five days later the crowd shouted again, only this time they screamed for Jesus' execution.

So don't worry too much about not having your personal set of cheering fans. Remember that you do have one personal cheerleader who will never stop pulling for you: God.

Riff, raff, Riff, raff, ruff. We play football and never get enough.
— Early OU cheer

**Just like the sports stars, you do have
a personal cheerleader: God.**

LUCKY CHARMS

Read Isaiah 2:6-16.

"They are full of superstitions from the East; . . . they bow down to the work of their hands" (vv. 6b, 8b).

The Sooners of 2004 went undefeated during the regular season, blasted Colorado 42-3 in the Big 12 Championship, and wound up in the BCS Championship. Talent had a lot to do with that, but there was something else at play: a whole bag of rituals.

Writer Carter Strickland said of the '04 Sooners, "Throughout the Oklahoma football team is an undercurrent of ritualistic behavior that sometimes borders on funny to freaky." With a whole closet full of rituals, sophomore defensive end Larry Birdine visited both extremes. At least he was clean about it. Each night before a game, he shaved. "I just always want to have that clean feeling," he said of his shaving ritual. "You look good. Clean. You play good." During each game-day eve, a clean-shaven Birdine passed the hours watching cartoons, especially Tom and Jerry.

Offensive lineman Jammal Brown knew what Birdine meant when he talked about being clean. Before each game, Brown took a shower -- with Caress. "It has that sweet smell," he said.

Food played an important part in the team's pre-game preparations. Offensive lineman Chris Messner always made sure that the kitchen had plenty of Cinnamon Toast Crunch cereal for him to plough through before a game. Quarterback Jason White sat at the exact same spot for the team dinner each Friday just as defensive back Brandon Shelby always sat in the same seat on the team bus.

Defensive tackle Lynn McGruder revealed that some players threw up before every game. "I don't know how they do it," he said. "They just do it." Not 312-lb. offensive lineman Davin Joseph, though. He never threw up because he never ate a bite the day of a game. Not even for the night games.

Superstitions – such as those of some of the '04 Sooners -- can be quite benign. Nothing in the Bible warns us about the dangers inherent in walking under ladders or not putting our clothes on a certain way.

God is quite concerned, however, about superstition of a more serious nature such as using the occult to predict the future. Its danger for us is that we allow something other than God to take precedence in our lives; we in effect worship idols.

While most of us scoff at palm readers and psychics, we nevertheless risk being idol worshippers of a different sort. Just watch the frenzied reaction of fans when a movie star or a star football player shows up. Or consider how we often compromise what we know is right merely to save face or to gain favor in the workplace.

Superstition is the stuff of nonsense. Idol worshipping, however, is as real for us today as it was for the Israelites. It is also just as dangerous.

We're a superstitious team.

-- Larry Birdine

**Superstition in the form of idol worship
is alive and well today, occurring anytime
we venerate anything other than God.**

RUN FOR IT

Read John 20:1-10.

"Peter and the other disciple started for the tomb. Both were running, but the other disciple outran Peter and reached the tomb first" (vv. 3-4).

When Joe Washington ran the ball, he was easy to spot. He had silver shoes.

"Smoke through a keyhole." So did Texas head coach Darrell Royal describe Washington. From 1972-75, Little Joe Washington set a school record by rushing for 4,071 yards. (Billy Sims broke it with 4,118 yards.) It's been said of Washington that he "held the franchise on Sooner excitement." Maybe it was the shoes.

Prior to the 1972 Colorado game, OU quarterback Dan Ruster smelled paint in the bathroom. He stood on the toilet and stared down into the stall next to him to espy Washington spraying his white shoes with silver paint. When Ruster asked him what he was doing, Washington replied, "If I had sprayed them before we went out to warm up, the coaches would've told me to change them. Now before kickoff, they won't have time."

In the film room after the game, head coach Barry Switzer suddenly asked, "Little Joe! What are those things on your feet?" "Those are my silver shoes, Coach," he replied. "Oh, okay," Switzer said. That was all he said about them.

Switzer drew a lot of criticism, though, for running an undisciplined team because he let a single player wear silver shoes.

Before one game, Switzer said something to his star halfback about it. "What do you want me to do, Coach?" Washington asked. "Just put a couple of hundred on them today," Switzer replied. Washington rushed for 211 yards that day, and indignation about the silver shoes lessened.

The silver shoes actually didn't catch the head Sooner by surprise. Washington had started wearing silver shoes in high school, so Switzer knew he would probably wear them at OU. The coach didn't care what kind of shoes Washington wore, just as long as he was running to daylight in them.

Hit the ground running -- every morning that's what you do as you leave the house and re-enter the rat race. You run errands; you run though a presentation; you give someone a run for his money; you always want to be in the running and never run-of-the-mill.

You're always running toward something, such as your goals, or away from something, such as your past. Many of us spend much of our lives attempting to run away from God, the purposes he has for us, and the blessings he is waiting to give us.

No matter how hard or how far you run, though, you can never outrun yourself or God. God keeps pace with you, calling you in the short run to take care of the long run by falling to your knees and running for your life -- to Jesus -- just as Peter and the other disciple ran that first Easter morning.

On your knees, you run all the way to glory.

I don't care if he plays barefoot. Just give him the ball.
-- Barry Switzer on Joe Washington's silver shoes

You can run to eternity by going to your knees.

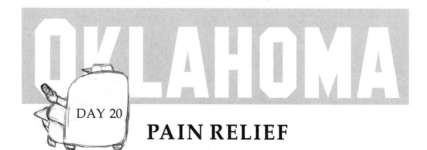

PAIN RELIEF

Read 2 Corinthians 1:3-7.

"Just as the sufferings of Christ flow over into our lives, so also through Christ our comfort overflows" (v. 5).

How's this for dealing with pain? Natasha Kelley competed for two seasons as one of the best collegiate gymnasts in the country with her right knee in two pieces all the while.

Three weeks before Kelley's freshman season of 2008 started at OU, she was working a routine when she felt a sharp pain on the back of her calf. "I thought the floor had broken," she said. As she lay on the matt, she looked for the busted shard of wood that her smacked her in the back of the leg. The floor was fine, her leg wasn't. She missed the season with a torn Achilles tendon.

Right before Thanksgiving of 2009, Kelley was working on a new skill, landed, and had her knee go sideways. "I felt it pop out, then pop back in," she said. Her ACL had snapped.

The doctor gave her a choice of surgery and the loss of another season, or rehabilitation and the possibility of competing. "That's what I'm doing," Kelley said, dismissing surgery. "You can't stop Nastasha," her mother declared.

When the swelling went down in her knee, Kelley went back into the gym. She discovered she could do her routines on the uneven bars, the balance beam, and the vault -- without an ACL.

"If I sat back and thought about somebody competing without an ACL," Kelley said, "I'd probably be like, 'Oh, that's not possible.'" But she got used to the pain the routines required, though head coach K.J. Kindler admitted that what she did was "extremely rare." In fact, as Kelley said, "It doesn't seem like as much of a big deal to me because it seems like it's normal." But it wasn't.

And how did she do, performing high-level gymnastics with a torn ACL? She made All-Big 12 in 2010 and 2011 and All-America in 2011, winning seventeen individual event titles, including the Big 12 championship on the beam in 2011 and an NCAA Regional championship on bars in 2011. Those two seasons were the best in OU's history at the time with a runner-up finish in 2010.

Since you live on Earth and not in Heaven, you are forced to play with pain as Natasha Kelley did. Whether it's a car wreck that left you shattered, the end of a relationship that left you battered, or a loved one's death that left you tattered -- pain finds you and challenges you to keep going.

While God's word teaches that you will reap what you sow, life also teaches that pain and hardship are not necessarily the result of personal failure. Pain in fact can be one of the tools God uses to mold your character and change your life.

What are you to do when you are hit full-speed by the awful pain that seems to choke the very will to live out of you? Where is your consolation, your comfort, and your help?

In almighty God, whose love will never fail. When life knocks you to your knees, you're closer to God than ever before.

I've always been pretty good with pain.
-- Natasha Kelley on competing with a torn ACL

When life hits you with pain, you can always turn to God for comfort, consolation, and hope.

DAY 21

BE KIND

Read Ephesians 4:25-32.

"Be kind and compassionate to one another, forgiving each other, just as in Christ God forgave you" (v. 32).

Darrell Royal always wished he had thanked the policeman who put him in jail.

Royal is a college football legend. He played defensive back and quarterback on the 10-1 OU team of 1948 and quarterback on the undefeated 1949 team that beat LSU 35-0 in the Sugar Bowl.

"Considered one of the greatest all-around players in Sooners history," Royal was All-America in '49. His total of eighteen career interceptions is still the school record. He was inducted into the College Football Hall of Fame in 1983 and the Oklahoma Sports Hall of Fame in 2000.

Royal's father took the family to California in 1939 in search of work, which seemed to end young Darrell's dream of playing football for OU. But when his high school football coach wrote and told the teenager he had a job for him if he would come back to Hollis and play ball, the youngster hit the road, hitchhiking back home to Oklahoma.

He was stranded in Abilene and crawled behind some bushes in front of the courthouse to sleep for the night. A bright light in his face awakened him. A policeman had discovered him, and the officer was convinced what he had found was a runaway.

Royal explained to the policeman he was on his way to get a

job his football coach had promised him. He then produced the letter that proved he was telling the truth. The policeman led him into one of the cells in the courthouse and let him sleep the night there on a cot. "They didn't lock it," Royal said. The next morning, Royal ate breakfast with the prisoners. The policeman then drove him to the highway so he could catch a ride. Thanks to the kindness of a stranger, Darrell Royal was on his way again.

We may all talk about kindness, but moving beyond the talk to demonstrating kindness to others is so exceptional in our world that we take notice of it. The person who finds a wallet with cash in it and returns it to the owner merits a spot on the evening news. So does the millionaire who gives a big chunk of change to a hospital or a charity.

Practicing kindness is difficult because it requires us to move beyond ourselves to an awareness of the needs of others and a willingness to do something about those needs without any expectation of blessings in return. A kind person places others first.

In an impersonal and often cruel and indifferent world, a kind person goes to the time and the trouble to establish personal contact—just as Jesus did. It was God himself, though, who undertook the kindest act in all of history by sending Jesus to us.

All these years, I wished I would have gotten [the policeman's] name so I could have written him to thank him for his kindness.

— Darrell Royal

**Practicing kindness is hard
because it requires us to place others first,
exactly the way Jesus lived among us.**

TEST CASE

Read James 1:2-12.

"Blessed is the man who perseveres under trial, because when he has stood the test, he will receive the crown of life that God has promised to those who love him" (v. 12).

The Sooners aced what their head coach called "a great test" and thus took the league title and a berth in the Orange Bowl.

For most of the afternoon of Nov. 22, 1986, the 8-2 Nebraska Cornhuskers played as though they had plans to derail the 9-1 Sooners' march to yet another Big Eight championship. With a touchdown early in the second half, Nebraska led 17-7.

From there, though, Oklahoma's top-ranked defense shut the Huskers down completely. "Intimidation," was the way All-American linebacker Brian Bosworth described what happened.

The offense still struggled, however, committing three last-half turnovers that apparently doomed OU to its second defeat of the season. With only 4:10 to play and Nebraska leading 17-10, the stalwart defense forced yet another Nebraska punt. Thus began what head Sooner Barry Switzer referred to as "a great test."

When sophomore quarterback Jamelle Holieway trotted onto the field to begin that test, he faced 94 yards of real estate. What followed was a drive that still holds a place in Oklahoma football lore. The big play was a 35-yard pass to Derrick Shepard to the Nebraska 32. Seconds later, Holieway found All-American tight end Keith Jackson with a 17-yard TD toss. With 1:22 on the clock,

SOONERS

the game was tied.

When that intimidating defense forced a three-and-out, the Sooners set up their test-taking station at their own 35. On third down, Jackson made a one-handed grab of a Holieway pass and got out of bounds with six seconds left at the Nebraska 14. Tim Lashar booted a 31-yard game-winning field goal.

The Sooners had a 20-17 win and a test grade of "A+." Having watched their team flunk its own test, the Nebraska crowd sat in shocked silence.

Life often seems to be one battery of tests after another: high-school and college final exams, college entrance exams, the driver's license test, professional certification exams. They all stress us out because they measure our competency, and we fear that we will be found wanting.

But it is the tests in our lives that don't involve paper and pen that often demand the most of us. That is, like the Sooners, we regularly run headlong into challenges, obstacles, and barriers that test our abilities, our persistence, and our faith.

Life itself is one long test, which means some parts are bound to be hard. Viewing life as an ongoing exam may help you keep your sanity, your perspective, and your faith when troubles come your way. After all, God is the proctor, but he isn't neutral. He even gave you the answer you need to pass with flying colors; that answer is "Jesus."

We've done it so many times that we believe if we stay close, we can win any ballgame.
-- Barry Switzer on being tested and overcoming

Life is a test that God wants you to ace.

TEST CASE   45

PRAYER WARRIORS

Read Luke 18:1-8.

"Then Jesus told his disciples a parable to show them that they should always pray and not give up" (v. 1).

P lease, dear Lord, don't let the best team win." What happened after that was indeed an answer to that most unusual and legendary Oklahoma prayer.

In October 1976, Barry Switzer's record as the OU head football coach was an eye-popping 36-1-1, but this month was not to be kind to him or his team. The Sooners tied Texas 6-6 when the snap on the extra point attempt was high, and they later lost to Oklahoma State and Colorado.

It seemed as though the Sooners were on their heels when they traveled to Lincoln for the season finale. In reality, they were 7-2-1 and with a win could tie for the league title. Nevertheless, "that day at Lincoln, OU seemed outmanned." Perhaps that realization inspired team captain and all-conference defensive back Scott Hill to offer up perhaps the most famous pre-game prayer in OU history: "Please, dear Lord, don't let the best team win."

Whether it did or not remains subject to debate. What isn't subject to discussion is that the game was yet another memorable one in a long line of great games between the two powerhouses.

Nebraska was apparently in control with a 17-13 lead, three minutes left to play, and OU sitting at its own 16. But sophomore Woodie Shepard threw a halfback pass to freshman end Steve

SOONERS

Rhodes for a 50-yard gain to give some life to the Sooner cause.

On third and 19, OU pulled off yet another trick play. Backup quarterback Dean Blevins hit Rhodes with a short pass; Rhodes then pitched the ball to the trailing halfback, Elvis Peacock, who sprinted to the 3. The Cornhuskers didn't have a prayer after that; Peacock scored with less than a minute on the clock.

The 20-17 Sooner win was an answer to many a prayer.

Scott Hill and his Sooner teammates prayed and then didn't give up. That's exactly what Jesus taught us to do as his followers: always pray and never give up.

Any problems we may have with prayer and its results derive from our side, not God's. We pray for a while about something – perhaps fervently at first – but our enthusiasm wanes if we don't receive the answer we want exactly when we want it. Why waste our time by asking for the same thing over and over again?

But God isn't deaf; God does hear our prayers and God does respond to them. As Jesus clearly taught, our prayers have an impact because they turn the power of Almighty God loose in this world. Thus, falling to our knees and praying to God is not a sign of weakness and helplessness. Rather, praying for someone or something is an aggressive act, an intentional ministry, a conscious and fervent attempt on our part to change someone's life or the world for the better.

God responds to our prayers; we often just can't perceive or don't understand how he is making those prayers come about.

You can do two things with your head down: play golf and pray.
-- Lee Trevino

Jesus taught us to always pray and never give up.

BLESS YOU

Read Romans 5:1-11.

"We also rejoice in our sufferings because we know that suffering produces perseverance; perseverance, character; and character, hope. And hope does not disappoint us" (*vv. 3-5a*).

At Oklahoma, Francie Ekwerekwu faced something new in her life: time on the bench. She eventually saw it as a great blessing.

Ekwerekwu finished her volleyball career at OU in 2010 with a senior season shortened by injuries. Otherwise, she was a starter for four seasons and was named to the All-Big 12 Academic Team four times.

The genial Texan early on became a crowd favorite appreciated for her tireless leadership and hustle. Ekwerekwu saw herself as more than just a leader on the court, however. "Volleyball has given me such a wonderful platform from which to share Jesus," she said. "My teammates look to me as a spiritual leader, and every chance I get I try to feed them God."

Ekwerekwu found herself tested, though, when she arrived in Norman in 2006. For the first time in her life, she wasn't playing. She was on the bench, fourth on the depth chart, a situation that ultimately led her to be redshirted.

"It was really tough," she said, "because I went from being a starter in every sport I played in high school to playing only one sport in college and being the last member of the roster. It was really humbling." In her humility, Ekwerekwu leaned more than ever before on God.

She found it all to be a blessing in disguise. She came to understand that her mentality should not be aimed at getting onto the court because that would prove her coaches wrong but rather that it would prove God right. "That's when things really started becoming uplifting," she said.

That redshirt season gave Ekwerekwu another blessing. She had time to become involved with the Fellowship of Christian Athletes.

We just never know what God is up to. We can know, though, that he's always busy preparing blessings for us and that if we trust and obey him, he will pour out those blessings upon us.

Those blessings, however, sometimes come to us disguised as hardship and disappointment as was the case with Francie Ekwerekwu. Often in our own lives, it is only after we can look back upon what we have endured that we understand it as a blessing.

The key lies in trusting God, in realizing that God isn't out to destroy us but instead is interested only in doing good for us, even if that means allowing us to endure the consequences of a difficult lesson. God doesn't manage a candy store; more often, he relates to us as a stern but always loving father. If we truly love and trust God, no matter what our situation is now, he has blessings in store for us. This, above all, is our greatest hope.

Always have the attitude of gratitude and count your blessings.
-- Former NFL head coach Tony Dungy

Life's hardships are often transformed into blessings when we endure them trusting in God.

WINNER'S CIRCLE

Read 1 John 5:1-12.

"Who is it that overcomes the world? Only he who believes that Jesus is the Son of God" (v. 5).

With practically everyone in the known world recruiting Adrian Peterson, how do you separate yourself from the pack? If you're Oklahoma, you talk about winning.

Peterson, of course, is an OU legend who exploded onto college football in 2004 as no freshman ever had before. He rushed for 1,925 yards, an NCAA freshman record. He was a first-team All-America, and became the first freshman in college football history to finish as the runner-up for the Heisman Trophy.

Injuries cost Peterson considerable playing time his sophomore and junior seasons. He then turned pro. Despite that shortened time in Norman, Peterson rushed for 4,045 yards, only 73 yards short of all-time OU rushing leader Billy Sims.

Peterson was no secret in high school, and Texas seemed to be the obvious choice. He was raised there; his uncle was a defensive end there in the '90s; he even had a poster of Texas running back Ricky Williams in his room. He was also subjected to some local pressure such as a full-page newspaper ad urging him to stay in the state.

But OU running backs coach Cale Gundy got Peterson's attention with an unconventional but effective approach. He didn't flatter the youngster, frankly admitting that the Sooners wanted

SOONERS

him. "But I'll tell you this," Gundy said. "We've won more games in the last five years than any other school in the country, and we're gonna keep winning whether you come here or not. You can join us or be on the other side."

Peterson then got a look at what life on the other side was like when he was OU's guest for the 2003 Texas game. Oklahoma won 65-13. Peterson chose the winning side.

Life itself, not just athletic events, is a competition. You vie against other job applicants. You seek admission to a college with a limited number of open spots. You compete against others for a date. Sibling rivalry is real; just ask your brother or sister.

Inherent in any competition or in any situation that involves winning and losing is an antagonist. You always have an opponent to overcome, even if it's an inanimate video game, a golf course, or even yourself.

Nobody wants to be numbered among life's losers. We recognize them when we see them, and maybe mutter a prayer that says something like, "There but for the grace of God go I."

But one adversary will defeat us: Death will claim us all. We can turn the tables on this foe, though; we can defeat the grave. A victory is possible, however, only through faith in Jesus Christ. With Jesus, we have hope beyond death because we have life.

With Jesus, we win. For all of eternity.

Winning means you're willing to go longer, work harder, and give more than anyone else.

-- Vince Lombardi

**Death is the ultimate opponent;
Jesus is the ultimate victor.**

AS A RULE

Read Luke 5:27-32.

"Why do you eat and drink with tax collectors and 'sinners'?" (v. 30b)

The Sooners seized upon changes in the rules that made passing the football easier. They threw for more than a mile in one season -- but would you believe it was in 1914?

In 1912, the national football rules committee completed its major overhaul of American football with a number of significant rules changes, among which was a repeal of the limitations on the forward pass. OU head coach Bennie Owen's obsession was speed, which the forward pass would take advantage of.

Already on hand, Owen had a freshman named Forest "Spot" Geyer. He had landed his nickname because a teammate said he "could throw a ball 50 yards and hit a nickel with it every time." Because Geyer could hit the spot, a classic OU nickname was born.

So was a legend. Nobody had ever seen anything like Geyer, who as a sophomore in 1913 "was successfully slinging the ball down the gridiron, thereby terrorizing heavier opponents such as the Nebraska Cornhuskers."

Geyer operated as a halfback out of a deep punt formation. (He also handled the kicking chores.) The Sooners perfected the end sweep in 1914. Geyer always had the option of faking the run and then throwing on the run. He was unstoppable, so much so that the Sooners threw the football for more than a mile that season.

The 9-1-1 record of 1914 was only a prelude to the first great season in OU history, though. Behind Geyer's pinpoint passing, the 1915 team went 10-0, once even scoring 102 points. Against Kansas that season, Geyer threw for 288 yards.

This remarkable All-American passer who used changes in the rules to play in a manner decades ahead of his time was inducted into the College Football Hall of Fame in 1973.

You live by rules that others set up. Some lender determined the interest rate on your mortgage and your car loan. You work hours and shifts somebody else established. Someone else decided what day your garbage gets picked up and what school district your house is in.

Jesus encountered societal rules also, including a strict set of religious edicts that dictated what company he should keep, what people, in other words, were fit for him to socialize with, talk to, or share a meal with. Jesus ignored the rules, choosing love instead of mindless obedience and demonstrating his disdain for society's rules by mingling with the outcasts, the lowlifes, the poor, and the misfits.

You, too, have to choose when you find yourself in the presence of someone whom society deems undesirable. Will you choose the rules or love? Are you willing to be a rebel for love — as Jesus was for you?

Oklahoma was the first team in America to rely on the forward pass.
-- Writer Brent Clark on OU's use of the rules changes of 1912

Society's rules dictate who is acceptable
and who is not, but love in the name of Jesus
knows no such distinctions.

BELIEVE IT

Read John 3:16-21.

"For God so loved the world that He gave His only begotten Son, that whoever believes in Him should not perish but have everlasting life" (v. 16 NKJV).

The drive to the 2000 national championship actually started before the season did -- when the Sooner players began to believe.

When he took over the OU football program in 1998, Bob Stoops immediately went after Josh Heupel to quarterback his spread offense. The junior-college QB had one question for Stoops: "Can we win the Big 12 championship and the national championship in my time at Oklahoma?" In other words, in two seasons. Stoops replied, "Yes, we could." The answer didn't impress Heupel so much as the fact that Stoops believed what he said.

Almost two years later, on a sweltering August afternoon, Heupel, now a senior and the Sooners' starting quarterback, didn't like the lackluster practice his team had just walked through. So in a meeting room inside the Barry Switzer Center, Heupel surprised his teammates by stepping out of character and delivering "an emotional exhortation. His voice rose, then cracked. His eyes misted."

What was it that inspired the normally staid quarterback to bare his soul? His belief that this team could win the national championship. Before the season started, Josh Heupel proclaimed the Sooners to be legitimate title contenders.

SOONERS

"It was his dream," said senior linebacker Roger Steffen. "It wasn't just a little pep talk. It was something he believed in. And he made everybody else in the room believe along with him."

"That's probably where this whole season started," said defensive tackle Jeremy Wilson-Guest. Right there on that hot afternoon when the Sooners first believed.

It ended on the floor of the Orange Bowl with the final leg of a journey that took that belief all the way to reality.

What we believe underscores everything about our lives. Our politics. How we raise our children. How we treat other people. Whether we respect others, their property and their lives.

Often, competing belief systems clamor for our attention; we all know persons – maybe friends and family members – who lost Christianity in the shuffle and the hubbub.

We turn aside from believing in Christ at our peril, however, because the heart and soul, the very essence of Christianity, is belief. That is, believing that this man named Jesus is the very Son of God and that it is through him – and only through him – that we can find forgiveness and salvation that will reserve a place for us with God.

But believing is more than simply acknowledging intellectually that Jesus is God. Even the demons who serve Satan know that. It is belief so deep that we entrust our lives and our eternity to Christ. We live like we believe it – because we do.

You could tell he really meant it and believed that we could get there.
-- Tackle Jeremy Wilson-Guest on Josh Heupel's August meeting

**Believe it: Jesus is the way – and the only way –
to eternal life with God.**

NOISEMAKER

Read Psalm 100.

"Shout for joy to the Lord, all the earth!" (v. 1)

Can a noisy crowd really be the difference in a basketball game? Oklahoma State's head coach sure thought so.

On Feb. 4, 2007, the ninth-ranked Oklahoma women's basketball team hosted OSU in their latest incarnation of Bedlam. Since it was Super Bowl Sunday, expectations generally were that the crowd wouldn't be as large as the 10,000 or so bodies the women had been averaging.

So much for expectations. The OU ladies wound up playing in front of the second-largest home crowd in the program's history. Just under 12,000 fans -- officially classified as a sell-out -- showed up for the game. The walk-up gate was so large that OU officials sold what amounted to standing-room-only tickets because all the seats were taken.

The crowd came ready to yell for their Sooners, too. State head coach Kurt Budke said after the game he thought the crowd was worth a good ten to fifteen points. "I think it was worth every bit of that tonight," he said. Which means the noisy, raucous crowd was the difference in the game. OU won 78-63.

It wasn't easy, though. The 17-3 Sooners were coming off back-to-back losses in which their play was characterized as "sloppy and sluggish." They started out the same way, falling behind 25-16 ten minutes into the game.

SOONERS

But head coach Sherri Coale and the home crowd weren't in the mood to let this game go the way of the last two. Coale stood up on the sideline and screamed one word to her players on the floor: "Fight!" After that, the team started playing with more intensity, and the crowd got into it, which added fuel to the fire.

The Sooners exploded for a 19-2 run that gave them a 35-27 lead at halftime. They finished with their 17th straight win in the series and their 11th straight victory by double digits.

Which really was a crowd pleaser.

Whether you're at an Oklahoma game live or watching on TV, no doubt you've contributed to the crowd noise generated by tens of thousands of fans or just your buddies. You've probably been known to whoop it up pretty good at some other times in your life, too. The birth of your first child. The concert of your favorite band. That fishing trip when you caught that big ole bass.

But how many times have you ever let loose with a powerful shout to God in celebration of his love for you? Though God certainly deserves it, he doesn't require that you walk around waving pompoms and shouting "Yay, God!" He isn't particularly interested in having you arrested as a public menace.

No, God doesn't seek a big show or a spectacle. A simple little "thank you" is quite sufficient when it's delivered straight from the heart and comes bearing joy. That kind of noise carries all the way to Heaven; God hears it even if nobody else does.

We have got to get used to executing when the crowd gets loud.
-- OSU freshman Andrea Riley after the OU game

The noise God likes to hear is a heartfelt
"thank you," even when it's whispered.

GOOD NEWS

Read Matthew 28:1-10.

'"He has risen from the dead and is going ahead of you into Galilee. There you will see him.' Now I have told you" (v. 7).

Steve Owens twice got some good news in unorthodox ways.

Owens' brothers drove the future All-American running back to Norman in the fall of 1966. They took a wrong turn and wound up driving through the entrance "of this big building where some older people were outside in heavy coats." Owens wondered if this were the university until one of his brothers said, "I think we're in the wrong place." They were at a mental institution.

Before long, Owens called his dad and told him he was coming back home. His father asked him where he was going to stay. "I thought I would stay with you all," Owens said. "Son, we don't have any room here," dad said. "You need to stay in Norman."

So Owens did and the rest is Sooner history and legend.

His sophomore season of '67, under new head coach Chuck Fairbanks, the team went 10-1, won the Big Eight title, and beat Tennessee in a thriller in the Orange Bowl. Owens didn't start the first three games, but he gained close to 100 yards in the opener and rushed for 129 yards in the 35-0 win over Maryland. In the 9-7 loss to Texas, he had 106 yards on 15 carries.

After that game, Owens received some good news, though no one officially delivered it to him. He simply found a first-team

SOONERS

jersey in his locker. He was a starter.

As Owens' senior season of 1969 wore down, he was a finalist for the Heisman Trophy. He was to sit by the phone at a pre-arranged time and wait for a call. His wife and he dutifully waited in the Student Union until ten minutes past the designated time. Owens then decided he didn't win and had waited long enough.

As they were leaving, a student hollered from upstairs, "Hey, Steve, you just won the Heisman!" That's how he got the news.

The story of mankind's "progress" through the millennia could be summarized and illustrated quite well in an account of how we disseminate our news. For much of recorded history, we told our stories through word of mouth, which required time to spread across political and geographical boundaries. That method also didn't do much to ensure accuracy.

Today, though, our news – unlike those two big news flashes delivered to Steve Owens-- is instantaneous. Yesterday's news is old news; we want to see it and hear about it as it happens.

But the biggest news story in the history of the world goes virtually unnoticed every day by the so-called mainstream media. It is, in fact, often treated as nothing more than superstition. But it's true, and it is the greatest, most wonderful news of all.

What headline should be blaring from every news source in the world? This one: "Jesus Rises from Dead, Defeats Death." It's still today's news, and it's still the most important news story ever.

Did the boy win that there trophy?
-- Steve Owens' dad, calling from a truck stop after hearing a rumor

The biggest news story in history took place when Jesus Christ walked out of that tomb.

DAY 30

MISSING IN ACTION

Read Luke 24:44-53.

"While he was blessing them, he left them and was taken up into heaven" (v. 51).

Losing his starting spot to an ankle injury was hard enough for Frank Alexander. Worse than that, though, was the absence of his father at his games.

The Monday morning after OU's 27-24 win over Air Force on Sept. 18, 2010, Alexander's mother called him with the horrible news that his father had had a heart attack. She told her son, "The best thing you can do for your dad right now is continue to do what you do." That is, play football.

That was hard. His family had always attended everything he played from the time he started with tee ball when he was 2. At high school playoff games, he often had fifty family members in the stands. There were always three. His mother said once in an interview, "We tell him that even if nobody else in the crowd is cheering for you, your mom, dad and sister are there."

But not now, and Alexander struggled with their absence as well as losing his starting defensive end spot because an injured ankle stubbornly refused to heal. "It was harder for him than for me and his little sister," his mom said.

But on Oct. 8, 2011 as Alexander ran down the tunnel in the Cotton Bowl to warm up for the Texas game, there was his father, waving his arms, raising his hands, and grabbing his son's attention with his unique whistle. "God has allowed me to come back and watch him," the elder Alexander said about his son.

With dad watching, Alexander had a monster game in the 55-17 humiliation of the Longhorns: three sacks, four tackles for loss, one forced fumble, one recovered fumble. "It can't get any better, to tell you the truth," his father said after congratulating his son. If only because his dad was there, Frank would agree.

The old saying claims, "Out of sight, out of mind," but we who love others as Frank Alexander loves his father know that the truer aphorism is "Absence makes the heart grow fonder."

Consider this, though: We spend our lives physically apart from our Jesus, the one we should love most of all. We don't get to walk down the street with him or have a cup of coffee with him. We never get to show him pictures of our children or talk Sooner football with him around the backyard grill.

As a result, too many people can't handle Jesus' physical absence, and they pretty much forget about him. Often we who still love him are careless and sometimes indifferent in our relationship. But Jesus never allows the flame that is his love for us even to flicker. Isn't that the way it is when one person truly loves another, no matter what the physical distance between them?

Missing Jesus so much that at times the pain seems physical is simply a symptom of our love for him.

He could've died. That's why I feel everything has just been a blessing.
-- Frank Alexander on having his dad back at his games

We are physically apart from Jesus, so which is it:
"Out of sight, out of mind" or
"Absence makes the heart grow fonder"?

STOP, THIEF!

Read Exodus 22:1-15.

"A thief must certainly make restitution" (v. 2b).

The Selmon brothers are football legends, but they turned out to be pretty good detectives, too. As well as judge and jury.

Lucious, Dewey, and Lee Roy Selmon (See Devotion No. 69.) played together only one season, 1973. Not surprisingly, considering their size and their rectitude, they were the self-appointed keepers of law and order in the athletic dorms.

Jay Upchurch tells the story that a problem occurred that year with thefts. Several items went missing from some of the players' rooms. The Selmon brothers determined they would uncover the thief and deal with him. They set out, therefore, on an in-house investigation.

Only a few days after the brothers began their detective work, a halfback from Houston didn't answer the roll call for one of head coach Barry Switzer's team meetings. Switzer called the player's name several times before he stopped and asked where he was. A player stood up and said, "He's on a bus back to Houston, Coach."

That certainly surprised Switzer, who asked the logical question: Why? The player explained that the Selmon brothers had "felt like it was the best thing for him to go back home" and had taken him down to the bus station.

It seems the Selmons had been quite successful in their investigation into the dorm thefts, uncovering some clues as to a pos-

SOONERS

sible suspect. The lock on the door of their target's dorm room didn't stymie them. They simply took the door off its hinges and discovered all of the stolen items in his closet.

Switzer explained what happened after that. "When they saw it was him, they packed his bags and drove him to the bus station. That was all that needed to be said."

Case closed.

Buckle up your seat belt. Wear a bicycle or motorcycle helmet. Use your pooper scooper to clean up after your dog. Don't walk on the grass. Picky ordinances, picky laws – in all their great abundance, they're an inescapable part of our modern lives.

When Moses came stumbling down Mt. Sinai after spending time as God's secretary, he brought with him a whole mess of laws and regulations, many of which undoubtedly seem picky to us today. What some of them provide, though, are practical examples of what for God is the basic principle underlying the theft of personal property: what is wrong must be made right.

While most of us today won't have to worry too much about the theft of livestock such as oxen, sheep, and donkeys, making what is wrong right remains a way of life for Christians. To get right with other people requires anything from restitution to apologies. To get right with God requires Jesus Christ.

Baseball is a sport where stealing is legal and you can spit anywhere you like, except in the umpire's eye or on the ball.
-- Legendary sportswriter Jim Murray

To make right the wrong of stealing requires restitution; to make right our relationship with God requires Jesus Christ.

GLORY DAYS

Read Psalm 96.

*"Ascribe to the Lord glory and strength. Ascribe to the
Lord the glory due his name" (vv. 7b, 8a).*

Sam Hazewinkel was just off the most disappointing loss of
his wrestling career. Yet there he was smiling and clowning with
a volleyball. Perhaps it was because he didn't wrestle for his own
glory, but for God's.

From 2003-2007, Hazewinkel was a four-time All-America at
Oklahoma. He placed third in the NCAA championships three
straight years before finishing second his senior year. He was a
gold medalist at the 2008 University World Games.

Hazewinkel didn't lose many times while he was a Sooner. His
sophomore season, for instance, he was 35-0 heading into the Big
12 finals against a wrestler he had already beaten. To everyone's
shock, he lost in overtime.

The loss could well have been devastating to most wrestlers,
but Hazewinkel never was any ordinary wrestler. He was raised
in a wrestling family; his dad and an uncle both wrestled for the
U.S. in the 1968 and '72 Olympics. More importantly, though, he
was raised in a Christian family. "Living a Christ-like life was
considered to be Number One in our house," Hazewinkel said.
"Christianity helps guide my life, helps me discover what I need
to do whenever there's a challenge."

So that guidance let him put the disappointing loss behind

him and move on to preparing for the NCAA championships. That's why a short time after his loss, he was carefree at practice, laughing and dunking over teammate Jake Hagar in the wrestlers' version of basketball: played with a volleyball and a 7-foot goal.

His faith took him not into recrimination but into the weight room and the video room and back to practice. He was getting ready for another match and another chance to give God the glory.

You may well remember the play that was your moment of athletic glory. Or the night you received an award from a civic group for your hard work. Your first (and last?) ace on the golf course. Your promotion at work. Your first-ever 10K race. Life does have its moments of glory.

But they amount to a lesser, transient glory, which actually harbors pain and disappointment as an integral part of it since you cannot recapture the moment. The excitement, the joy, even the happiness – they are fleeting; they pass as quickly as they arose, and you can never experience them again.

Glory days that last forever are found only through Jesus. That's because true glory properly belongs only to God, who has shown us his glory in Jesus. To accept Jesus into our lives is thus to take God's glory into ourselves. Glory therefore is an ongoing attribute of Christians. Our glory days are right now, and they will become even more glorious when Jesus returns.

I'm not out there wrestling for myself. I'm wrestling for the Lord.
-- Sam Hazewinkel

The glory of this earth is fleeting,
but the glory we find in Jesus lasts forever
– and will only get even more magnificent.

THE NIGHTMARE

Read Mark 5:1-20.

"What do you want with me, Jesus, Son of the Most High God? Swear to God that you won't torture me!" (v. 7)

For Curtis Lofton, Missouri's high-powered offense was his personal nightmare. So he went out and had a dream game.

Lofton had his doubters making the leap from a small high school to major college football. Sooner head coach Bob Stoops wasn't among them. "You project a guy for what he'll be able to do for you with his physical ability," he said. Lofton did a lot.

He started every game as a true freshman in 2005. In 2007, he was All-America and had the third highest number of tackles in the country. After the season, he turned pro.

On Oct. 13, 2007, the unbeaten, 11th-ranked Tigers roared into town with their spread offense that Lofton officially declared to be a middle linebacker's nightmare. It meant he would spend the afternoon in one-on-one coverage on speedy receivers and backs or in attempting open-field tackles.

Sure enough, the receivers came from everywhere as Missouri attempted 47 passes. Amid all the linebacker's terror was Lofton, who made sure the Tigers wound up with the bad dreams as the sixth-ranked Sooners won 41-31. In a performance that defensive coordinator Brent Venables called "outstanding," Lofton had eighteen tackles and a touchdown on a fumble return. The league named him its Big 12 Defensive Player of the Week.

Lofton's touchdown came on a fumbled exchange between the Missouri quarterback and a receiver in the fourth quarter. When Venables saw the play on tape, he saw more than just bad hands; he saw Lofton at work. "The receiver fumbles the ball on the sweep because he sees Curtis coming off the edge," Venables said. "So really, he kind of caused the fumble and scooped and scored."

When Missouri's nightmare was over, it was Lofton and his teammates who had the sweet dreams.

Falling. Drowning. Standing naked in a room crowded with fully dressed people. They're nightmares, dreams that jolt us from our sleep in anxiety or downright terror. The film industry has used our common nightmares to create horror movies that allow us to experience our fears vicariously. This includes the formulaic "evil vs. good" movies in which demons and the like render good virtually helpless in the face of their power and ruthlessness.

The spiritual truth, though, is that it is evil that has come face to face with its worst nightmare in Jesus. We seem to understand that our basic mission as Jesus' followers is to further his kingdom and change the world through emulating him in the way we live and love others. But do we appreciate that in truly living for Jesus, we are daily tormenting the very devil himself?

Satan and his lackeys quake helplessly in fear before the power of almighty God that is in us through Jesus.

I can't have a nightmare tonight. I've just lived through one.
-- Darrell Imhoff, the opposing center the night Wilt Chamberlain scored
100 points in an NBA game

As the followers of Jesus Christ,
we are the stuff of Satan's nightmares.

THE NIGHTMARE   67

THE BIG TIME

Read Matthew 2:19-23.

"He went and lived in a town called Nazareth" (v. 23).

The man who led Oklahoma football into the big time took on a program that had a long way to go.

When Bennie Owen came to Norman in 1905 to coach the OU football team, the athletic association was broke. It still owed two prior coaches -- Mark McMahan (1902-03) and Fred Ewing (1904) -- part of their salaries. OU football had no national reputation. The football field had only a wooden grandstand on one side that seated five hundred spectators.

The university needed a football genius, and they got one with a three-month contract for $900. "Nowhere in America was there a more skilled and creative football mind" than Owen. When the major rules changes of 1910 were instituted that created the game of football as we know it, he was ready.

Owen's teams became so good and so well known that in 1913, fullback and kicker Claude Reeds received enough national publicity to become the school's first All-America. Owen took Oklahoma into the Southwest Conference in 1915, and the team went 10-0. In 1920, he moved the Sooners into the Missouri Valley Conference and won the championship that first season. At the end of the 1920 season, Owen announced plans to build a football stadium, and by 1923, his vision resulted in Memorial Stadium circling Owen Field.

SOONERS

After the 1926 football season, though, Owen decided his time had come. He gave up the football team and stayed on as athletic director. In his 22 seasons, Owen's teams won 128 games and lost 52. He left the program on a sound financial footing with a roomy new stadium that drew fans from all over the region.

Bennie Owen had brought about the first golden age of Oklahoma football and in the process had moved the university and its team into big-time college athletics for good.

The move to the big time is one we often desire to make in our own lives. Bumps in the road, one-stoplight communities, and towns with only a convenience store, a church, and a voting place litter the American countryside.

Maybe you were born in one of them and grew up in a virtually unknown village in a backwater county. Perhaps you started out on a stage far removed from the bright lights of Broadway, the glitz of Hollywood, or the halls of power in Washington, D.C.

Those original circumstances don't have to define or limit you, though, for life is more than geography. It is about character and walking with God whether you're in the countryside or the city.

Jesus certainly knew the truth of that. After all, he grew up in a small town in an inconsequential region of an insignificant country ruled by foreign invaders.

Where you are doesn't matter. What you are does.

Who can Oklahoma play next? All southwestern teams are outclassed.
-- The Daily Oklahoman *in 1911 announcing big-time football at OU*

**Where you live may largely be the culmination
of a series of circumstances;
what you are is a choice you make.**

FAIL-SAFE

Read Luke 22:54-62.

"Peter remembered the word the Lord had spoken to him: 'Before the rooster crows today, you will disown me three times.' And he went outside and wept bitterly" (vv. 61b-62).

He quit the football team twice, threw nineteen interceptions and only nine touchdowns, and was booed on his home field. Yet, this "failure" was one of OU's greatest quarterbacks.

As a freshman in 1976, J.C. Watts was the seventh-string quarterback. "My first months in Norman were pretty rough," he admitted. Discouraged, he left the team twice.

The second time Watts went home, head coach Barry Switzer called him, told him to come back and talk to him, and "if you still want to leave after that, I will let you go." In the coach's office, Switzer told Watts exactly what his plans for him were: He would be redshirted in 1977, the backup in 1978, and the starting quarterback after that. "I didn't think he was lying to me and I decided to stick around," Watts said.

It worked out exactly as Switzer had said it would with Watts starting as a junior in 1979. He struggled some, especially against Texas when he fumbled four times and threw three interceptions. But the team won the Big Eight title, and he was the MVP of the Orange Bowl.

Watts heard boos from the home folks early in the 1980 season, but the Sooners rallied from a slow start to win the Big Eight. He ended his OU career in spectacular fashion in the Orange Bowl. OU trailed FSU 17-10 with 2:37 left, and he took the Sooners on a 76-yard drive highlighted by a 42-yard pass to wide receiver Steve Rhodes. The score came on an 11-yard toss to Rhodes with 1:27 left. OU got the 18-17 win when Watts hit tight end Forrest Valora for the two-point conversion. Watts again was the game's MVP.

Persevering through frustration and moments of failure, Watts was 22-3 as Oklahoma's starting quarterback.

Failure is usually defined by expectations, which for an OU starting quarterback run really high. A baseball player who hits .300 is a star, but he fails seventy percent of the time. We grumble about a postal system that manages to deliver billions of items without a hitch.

And we are often our own harshest critics, beating ourselves up for our failings because we expected better. Never mind that our expectations were unrealistic to begin with.

The bad news about life is that failure – unlike success -- is inevitable. Only one man walked this earth perfectly and we're not him. The good news about life, however, is that failure isn't permanent. In life, we always have time to reverse our failures as did Peter, he who failed our Lord so abjectly.

The same cannot be said of death. In death we eternally suffer the consequences of our failure to follow that one perfect man.

Because you fail doesn't make you a failure.

-- J.C. Watts

Only one failure in life dooms us to eternal failure in death: failing to follow Jesus Christ.

ON THE LIST

Read Exodus 20:1-17.

"God spoke all these words: 'I am the Lord your God . . . .
You shall have no other gods before me'" (vv. 1, 3).

As an OU football player, you did not want your name showing up on Biff Jones' list.

Jones arrived in Norman in 1935 after spending three seasons as the head man at LSU. He was a winner there with a 20-5-5 record. They were tumultuous years, though, that saw him gain notoriety by running Louisiana Gov. Huey P. Long out of the locker room at halftime of the '34 Tulane game.

Jones had served as captain of his team at West Point and had risen to the rank of major in the army. He had also served as head coach at West Point for four seasons. That military training, attitude, and outlook carried over into his coaching style. "He kind of ran the football team like it was army," said Barth Walker, a left guard from 1935-37.

Jones worked hard and was himself extremely disciplined. He was a no-nonsense guy and expected the same dedication from his players. He was distant from them, though. As Walker put it, "He hardly ever spoke to the players and basically sat back and let his assistants do their work."

But Jones did have a system for the occasions he wanted his players to know something. He posted it on a bulletin board. That board became a source of anxiety for the Sooner players.

SOONERS

At the end of Jones' first spring practice, he posted a list of names on that bulletin board with a heading that read: "The following players will not return next season." Jones and his coaches had analyzed every player and every position that spring and weeded out the young men whom they felt had no future as an OU football player.

"Your heart was basically in your throat," Walker said about walking up to that infamous board with its dreaded list. He quite obviously made the cut.

Like Biff Jones, you've got your list and you're ready to go: a gallon of paint and a water hose from the hardware store; chips, peanuts, and sodas from the grocery store for watching tonight's football game with your buddies; the tickets for the band concert. Your list helps you remember.

God also made a list once of things he wanted you to remember; it's called the Ten Commandments. Just as your list reminds you to do something, so does God's list remind you of how you are to act in your dealings with other people and with him.

A life dedicated to Jesus is a life devoted to relationships, and God's list emphasizes that the social life and the spiritual life of the faithful cannot be sundered. God's relationship to you is one of unceasing, unqualified love, and you are to mirror that divine love in your relationships with others. In case you forget, you have a list.

It was pretty scary walking up and looking at that list.
-- Barth Walker

God's list is a set of instructions on how you are to conduct yourself with other people and with him.

HEAD GAMES

Read Colossians 3:1-17.

"Set your mind on things above, not on earthly things" (v. 2).

Hollis Price was so tough physically that not even surgery to remove a piece of an opponent's tooth from his arm stopped him. But it was his mental toughness that really made him special.

For instance, Price missed a game his junior season of 2001-02 after he was poked in the eye during practice. He regarded the whole deal as a blessing. "Anytime I sit on the bench, I find myself coaching, and that's what I'd like to do eventually," he said.

A slight, 6'1" shooting guard, Price has been called "one of the best and most beloved Sooners." He was the leading scorer of the 2001-02 team that went 31-5, won the Big 12 Tournament, and advanced to the Final Four. He was first-team All-Big 12 and third team All-America that season.

That success required both physical and mental toughness. He played much of his sophomore season with a groin pull, but that was not nearly the most gruesome injury he suffered. He collided so forcefully with an opponent in the first round of the NCAA Tournament that the ulnar nerve in his right (shooting) arm was nearly severed. The tear was so severe that it required three surgeries to repair. One of them was to remove a piece of tooth.

Price's attitude about the injury that left his right arm so stiff he had to warm up 30 minutes before he could start playing? "It made me a better shooter because it made me focus more," he said.

Price had to develop that mental toughness to escape his childhood. He grew up in New Orleans' notorious Ninth Ward, the child of an absent father and a single mother who struggled with drug addiction. He fortunately had loving grandparents, people of faith who were strict but loving.

"I was one of the chosen ones," he said about escaping the mean streets of the projects. He was also one of the tough ones.

Once upon a time, survival required mere brute strength, but persevering in American society today generally necessitates mental strength rather than physical prowess.

Your job, your family, your finances -- they all demand mental toughness from you by placing stress upon you to perform. Stress is a fact of life, though it isn't all bad as we are often led to believe. Stress can lead you to function at your best. Rather than buckling under it, you stand up, make constant decisions, and keep going.

So it is with your faith life. "Too blessed to be stressed" sounds nice, but followers of Jesus Christ know all about stress. Society screams compromise; your children whine about being cool; your company ignores ethics. But you don't fold beneath the stress; you keep your mind on Christ and the way he said to live because you are tough mentally, strengthened by your faith.

After all, you have God's word and God's grace for relief and support.

He's not a big, strong kid, but mentally he's as tough as they come.
-- OU trainer Alex Brown on Hollis Price

Toughened mentally by your faith in Christ,
you live out what you believe, and you persevere.

DAY 38

PLAN AHEAD

Read Psalm 33:1-15.

"The plans of the Lord stand firm forever, the purposes of his heart through all generations" (v. 11).

Bob Stoops implemented his plan when he arrived in Norman in 1998. He got results faster than anybody expected -- except him.

After three straight losing seasons, the university regents voted in November 1998 to fire the head football coach. Eight days later, they hired Stoops away from the University of Florida.

From the first, Stoops had a plan. It included the spread offense, "a new, no-excuse attitude," an attention to detail, and a new work ethic. With that plan in mind, he hired his assistants, recruited his first Sooners, and "preached a new gospel to the Sooner faithful."

That message had nothing to do with rebuilding. When the new head man met with his team for the first time, he told them, "The time is now. We don't have time to rebuild. . . . It's a program of championships that should expect championships."

They were pretty words, but he was speaking of a program that despite its grand tradition had moved out of college football's penthouse. The Sooners had not played in January since the 1988 Citrus Bowl, had not appeared in a major bowl since the 1987 Orange Bowl, and had not won a bowl game since 1993.

So some players who heard were skeptical. Safety Ontei Jones said about that initial meeting, "Everyone was questioning, 'Is he for real?'" He was, and his players bought into it. "You could see there was something about him," said junior center Bubba Burcham. "More confidence. Higher expectations."

Though he had a plan, Stoops confessed, "I didn't know everything was going to work." Well, it did, and with such rapidity that everyone was dazzled -- except Stoops. In his second season, the Sooners were national champions. "We never had a date when we'd be in this position," he said after the 2000 season when his plan reached fruition. "But better sooner than later."

Like a successful football team, successful living takes planning. You go to school to improve your chances for a better job. You use blueprints to build your home. You plan for retirement. You map out your vacation to have the best time. You even plan your children -- sometimes.

Your best-laid plans, however, sometime get wrecked by events and circumstances beyond your control. The economy goes into the tank; a debilitating illness strikes; a hurricane hits. Life is capricious and thus no plans are foolproof.

But you don't have to go it alone. God has plans for your life that guarantee success as God defines it if you will make him your planning partner. God's plan for your life includes joy, love, peace, kindness, gentleness, and faithfulness, all the elements necessary for truly successful living for today and for all eternity. And God's plan will not fail.

I had some ideas about discipline and the way you do things and all, and after that you just sort of do the best you can every day.
-- Bob Stoops on his plan for OU football

Your plans may ensure a successful life;
God's plans will ensure a successful eternity.

SEEING THE VISION

Read Acts 26:1, 9-23.

"So then, . . . I was not disobedient to the vision from heaven" (v. 19).

George Lynn Cross was a visionary. The University of Oklahoma football program is the living proof.

Cross served as the university's president from 1943-68. Two years into his tenure, OU's football program was "floundering in poor health. It was on life support." OU had won only one conference championship since 1920. "What football trophies [the university] had were old and dusty." Following a 5-5 season in 1945, the head coach resigned.

At a regents meeting to discuss the hiring of a new coach, Dr. Cross revealed the depth and breadth of his vision for OU's football program. He realized that the university's football team "could serve as a centerpiece for camaraderie, pride, and enthusiasm among student, alumni, and all residents of the state." As Cross recalled it, "It was 1945, and the war had ended, and here in Oklahoma, we were still feeling very depressed from those tough days that Steinbeck wrote about in *The Grapes of Wrath*."

Years later, Barry Switzer said, "After the war, maybe when Oklahoma didn't have much to be proud of, George Cross and some other people said, 'Let's create something good, something that Oklahoma can be proud of.'" What Cross understood was that with the influx of talented athletes coming home from the war, the time was right to build such a program.

An athlete at South Dakota State, Cross was a sports fan, and he knew something about football. His vision encompassed the type of man needed to lead the program to greatness. Thus, he insisted that the new coach, Jim Tatum, bring along his assistant. A miffed Tatum complied; one year later he trucked off to Maryland and that assistant, Bud Wilkinson, was the new OU football coach.

George Lynn Cross's vision was on its way to becoming his greatest legacy.

To speak of visions is often to risk their being lumped with palm readings, Ouija boards, seances, horoscopes, and other such useless mumbo-jumbo. The danger such mild amusements pose, however, is very real in that they indicate a reliance on something other than God. It is God who knows the future; it is God who has a vision and a plan for your life; it is God who has the answers you seek as you struggle to find your way.

You probably do have a vision for your life, a plan for how it should unfold. It's the dream you pursue through your family, your job, your hobbies, your interests. But your vision inspires a fruitful life only if it is compatible with God's plan. As the apostle Paul found out, you ignore God's vision at your peril. But if you pursue it, you'll find an even more glorious life than you could ever have envisioned for yourself.

We want to build a university our football team can be proud of.
-- George Lynn Cross, asking the Oklahoma legislature for money

Your grandest vision for the future
pales beside the vision God has
of what the two of you can accomplish together.

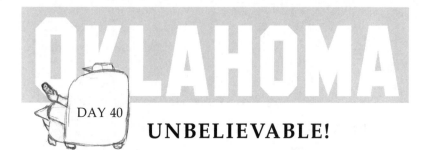

UNBELIEVABLE!

Read Hebrews 3:7-19.

"See to it, brothers, that none of you has a sinful, unbelieving heart that turns away from the living God" (v. 12).

Derland Moore's football story is so unbelievable than even OU assistant coach Barry Switzer was flabbergasted by him.

In the summer of 1969, Sooner track coach J.D. Martin served as an official at a high school track meet in Norman. He was surveying the athletes with a coach's eye when he saw all six-foot-five, 250-lbs of Derland Moore heave the shot impressive distances.

Martin introduced himself and to his surprise learned that Moore hadn't been recruited by anybody. Moreover, Moore said he wanted to throw but he really wanted to play football.

That sent Martin scurrying to a phone. He located freshman football coach Don Jimerson and asked him to give Moore a quick tour of the campus. "Just talk him into coming here and I'd give him a track scholarship," Martin said.

Before Moore climbed onto the bus to head home, he told Martin that if his dad was all right with it, he'd go to Oklahoma. Sure enough, Moore showed up that fall to play football.

As Switzer saw it, Moore played football but "was a track guy who somehow didn't attract a lot of attention." It took Moore only one practice at OU to attract attention. "All of a sudden he squatted down there and started beating people up," Switzer said.

SOONERS

He called Martin after the first practice to tell him he couldn't believe this walk-on was whipping his All-Americas.

But that was Derland Moore's unbelievable story. A walk-on defensive tackle, he received a scholarship his sophomore season and was a three-year starter, a two-time All-Big Eight player, and All-America as a senior in 1972. He was drafted in the second round by the Saints and had a 13-year pro career.

Much of what taxes the limits of our belief system has little effect on our lives. Maybe we don't believe in UFOs, honest politicians, aluminum baseball bats, Sasquatch, or the viability of electric cars. A healthy dose of skepticism is a natural defense mechanism that helps protect us in a world that all too often has designs on taking advantage of us.

That's not the case, however, when Jesus and God are part of the mix. Quite unbelievably, we often hear people blithely assert they don't believe in God. Or brazenly declare they believe in God but don't believe Jesus was anything but a good man and a great teacher.

At this point, unbelief becomes dangerous because God doesn't fool around with scoffers. He locks them out of the Promised Land, which isn't a country in the Middle East but Heaven itself.

Given that scenario, it's downright unbelievable that anyone would not believe.

That's unheard of. A walk-on who turned out to be a first- or second-round draft pick in the NFL. But Derland [Moore] was the real deal.
-- Barry Switzer

Perhaps nothing is as unbelievable as that some people insist on not believing in God or his son.

DAY 41

BEING DIFFERENT

Read Daniel 3.

*"We want you to know, O king, that we will not serve
your gods or worship the image of gold you have set up"
(v. 18).*

It took a horrible tragedy, but Keara Jones became a different person by becoming the person she used to be.

Two things were solid in Jones' world: her soccer and her faith. In 2000, though, that began to change when she was a freshman playing soccer at Southwest Baptist University. "I made a lot of poor decisions and pushed God off to the side," she said.

God refused to stay there. One horrible night spring semester, Jones and a group of friends went to a party that involved alcohol. Three of them were killed riding home. "God broke me down with that accident," she said. "He told me, 'You are not the same person who came here in August.' I wasn't."

The team trainer held a Bible study that week, and Jones went. "God tore me apart," she said of the worship that evening. "I've never cried as much as I did that night." She almost got kicked out of school and off the soccer team, but again God watched out for her. "Whoever turned me in (to school administrators for drinking) helped lead me back to Christ," she said.

So Keara Jones was a different person now.

In 2001, she decided to walk on at Oklahoma. It was hard. At Southwest, she had been the starter and honorable mention all-conference; at OU, she was number three. But in 2002, one goalie was injured and the other studied abroad. The reserve who was a different person from what she had been became a starter.

There was something else different about Keara Jones. She was born with a cataract in her right eye, rendering her legally blind in that eye. As one writer put it, the one-eyed goalie now had amazing vision in her life because of her renewed faith.

While we live in a secular society that constantly pressures us to conform to its principles and values, we serve a risen Christ who calls us to be different. Therein lies the great conflict of the Christian life in contemporary America.

But how many of us really consider that even in our secular society we struggle to conform as Keara Jones did? In a sense, we are all geeks. Thus, we can never truly conform because we were not created by God to live in such a sin-filled world in the first place. Thus, when Christ calls us to be different by following and espousing Christian beliefs, principles, and practices, he is summoning us to the lifestyle we were born for.

The most important step in being different for Jesus is realizing and admitting what we really are: We are children of God; we are Christians. Only secondarily are we citizens of a secular world. That world both scorns and disdains us for being different; Jesus both praises and loves us for it.

You can believe what you want to believe, but [Keara's] a different person. God has given peace in her life.
-- Keara Jones' mother to the Southwest Baptist Dean of Student Life

The lifestyle Jesus calls us to is different from that of the world, but it is the way we were born to live.

THE MAKEOVER

Read 2 Corinthians 5:11-21.

"If anyone is in Christ, he is a new creation; the old has gone, the new has come!" (v. 17)

Ryan Broyles' life was made over when he started reading the Good Book to go with his playbook.

Broyles is the most prolific wide receiver in NCAA history. On Oct. 15, 2011, he caught his 318th pass and thus broke the all-time career reception record previously held by Taylor Stubblefield of Purdue. His college career ended prematurely when he tore an ACL on Nov. 5 in OU's 41-25 win over Texas A&M, but he finished with 349 catches. He was a two-time All-America (2010-11).

Even while Broyles was apparently flourishing, though, he wasn't living as he should. "I was missing something," he said.

He was living the way he thought he should, the way a high-profile athlete lives. "I'm supposed to be cocky," he said. "I'm supposed to party. I'm supposed to love on girls. I was oblivious." He drank regularly at bars after games and during the off-season; he cursed nonstop; he listened to rap music, which he said only reinforced his bad behavior.

In the months prior to his junior season of 2010, Broyles began to question his lifestyle. "This isn't right; this isn't cool," he found himself thinking. There to reinforce the doubt he was feeling about the way he was living was his longtime girlfriend, who continually encouraged him to go to church. Broyles grew up in the church and identified himself as a Christian, but admitted later he really wasn't one. "I knew about God and Jesus, but I never had a relationship," he said.

But when his girlfriend bought him a Bible, Broyles read it faster then she was reading hers. He then started going to church regularly with her. He gave up the bars, the cursing, the rap music. In May 2011, he joined eight Sooner teammates on a Christian mission trip to Haiti.

Ryan Broyles was made over into a Christian in reality and not just in name.

Ever considered a makeover? TV shows show us how changes in clothes, hair, and makeup and some weight loss can radically alter the way a person looks. But these changes are only skin deep. Even with a makeover, the real you — the person inside — remains unchanged. How can you make over that part of you?

By giving your heart and soul to Jesus just as Ryan Broyles did. You won't look any different; you won't dance any better; you won't suddenly start talking smarter. The change is on the inside where you are brand new because the model for all you think and feel is now Jesus. He is the one you care about pleasing.

Made over by Jesus, you realize that gaining his good opinion — not the world's — is all that really matters. And he isn't the least interested in how you look but how you act.

Ryan has grown substantially. His personal conduct is exactly what you're looking for in a leader.
-- Head coach Bob Stoops on Ryan Broyles' makeover

Jesus is the ultimate makeover artist; he can make you over without changing the way you look.

COMEBACK KIDS

Read Luke 23:26-43.

"Jesus answered him, 'I tell you the truth, today you will be with me in paradise'" (v. 43).

Before the Sooners could win the 1975 national title, they had to do something most of them had never done before at Oklahoma: come back from a defeat.

On Nov. 8, 1975, the Sooners lost to Kansas 23-3. It was the first loss of Barry Switzer's head coaching career, and it came in his 31st game. Oklahoma had not been beaten on the field in 37 straight games. Quarterback Steve Davis was typical of many of the players. He was a senior in his next-to-last home game, and he had never before experienced defeat wearing an OU uniform.

The loss dropped the Sooners to seventh in the rankings. Coming so late in the season, it apparently doomed their chances of a repeat national title. They didn't help themselves the following week against Missouri. Only a legendary touchdown run by Joe Washington and a two-point conversion with a little more than three minutes left to play let the Sooners pull out a 28-27 win.

Against second-ranked and unbeaten Nebraska, though, the Sooners scored three times in the fourth quarter to win 35-10. The rout jumped OU back up to No. 3 in the polls. When No. 2 Texas A&M lost to Arkansas the next week, the comebacks kids were right back in the hunt for the national title.

They needed help and they got it. In the locker room before

they took the field against Michigan in the Orange Bowl, they learned top-ranked Ohio State had lost to UCLA. "Boy, this game got big all of a sudden," said offensive coordinator Galen Hall.

It did indeed. The Sooners only scored twice, but it was more than enough. Senior All-American receiver Billy Brooks scored from 40 yards out on a reverse pitch in the first half; Davis scored from 10 yards out in the third quarter. Oklahoma won 14-6.

The comeback from the awful loss was complete. The Sooners were national champions.

Life will have its setbacks whether they result from personal failures or from forces and people beyond your control. Being a Christian and a faithful follower of Jesus Christ doesn't insulate you from getting into deep trouble. Maybe financial problems suffocated you. A serious illness put you on the sidelines. Or your family was hit with a great tragedy.

Life is a series of victories and defeats. Winning isn't about avoiding defeat; it's about getting back up to compete again. It's about making a comeback of your own.

When you avail yourself of God's grace and God's power, your comeback is always greater than your setback. You are never too far behind, and it's never too late in life's game for Jesus to lead you to victory, to turn trouble into triumph. As it was with the Sooners of 1975 and the thief on the cross who repented, it's not how you start that counts; it's how you finish.

Hold your heads up. You are a great ballclub.
-- Barry Switzer to his players after the Kansas loss

In life, victory is truly a matter of how you finish and whether you finish with Jesus at your side.

SOMETHING NEW

Read Ephesians 4:17-24.

"You were taught . . . to put off your old self . . . and to put on the new self, created to be like God in true righteousness and holiness" (vv. 22, 24).

When Oklahoma played its first-ever collegiate football game, the sport was so new that the local sheriff mistook it for a drunken brawl and tried to break it up.

As the university's first official football team with its first-ever football coach took the field in 1897, no equipment existed for this brand new game. Each player had to find his own. They fashioned crude football shoes by nailing leather cleats to heavy brogans. No OU player had a helmet until Joe Merkle employed a local harness maker to fashion one out of leather. The other players simply let their hair grow long for protection.

This new game was crude and violent, "a game of brute force" with no passing, no finesse, and no deception. Nevertheless, the public loved it. At the first game in 1897 (See Devotion No. 86.), which OU won 16-0, enthusiastic fans and students "scaled the fence encircling the field in order to embrace the varsity players." The problem was they did this continually during the second half, running right onto the field in the middle of play.

The newness of football was never demonstrated more clearly than on Dec. 31, 1897, when the team made its first-ever road trip and played its first-ever intercollegiate game. The opponent was

Kingfisher College with the game at the Guthrie fairground.

The OU varsity was on its way to a 17-8 win and the completion of the school's first undefeated season when the Logan County sheriff showed up. Not surprisingly, he had never seen a football game before, and he -- somewhat logically -- mistook the melee for a drunken brawl. He pulled his pistol, ran onto the field, and halted play. Only an earnest and extended explanation from OU President David Ross Boyd convinced the constable that the boys were actually engaged in a newfangled game.

New things in our lives often have a life-changing effect. A new spouse. A new baby. A new job. Even something as mundane as a new television set or lawn mower jolts us with change.

While new experiences, new people, and new toys may make our lives new, they can't make new lives for us. Inside, where it counts – down in the deepest recesses of our soul – we're still the same, no matter how desperately we may wish to change. The new stuff doesn't change the old us.

An inner restlessness drives us to seek escape from a life that is a monotonous routine. Such a mundane existence just isn't good enough for someone who is a child of God; it can't even be called living. We want more out of life; something's got to change.

The only hope for a new life lies in becoming a brand new man or woman. And that is possible only through Jesus Christ, he who can make all things new again.

I was feeling kind of blue, but I had liked the rough physical contact.
-- Jap Clapam after the first OU football game

A brand new you with the promise of a life worth living is waiting in Jesus Christ.

ATTITUDE CHECK

Read 1 Thessalonians 5:12-22.

"Give thanks in all circumstances, for this is God's will for you in Christ Jesus" (v. 18).

Jessica Shults developed a new attitude about playing softball. Almost losing the game you love will do that to you.

In 2011, Shults, the team's sophomore catcher, was a star for yet another Oklahoma team on its way to the College World Series. "She was definitely one of the best out there," said legendary OU softball coach Patty Gasso. Shults was playing so well that with much of the season still to go, she was only two home runs shy of setting a new school single-season record. And it all went wrong.

As the season wore on, Shults was in agony from a growing pain in her abdomen and she didn't know why. She could no longer eat and the pain was kept her awake at night. As a result, she grew weaker and her impressive numbers on the field dipped.

Her attitude changed, too. Gasso noticed it. "When she is not herself, it is very evident," she said. "She was a little more quiet, not as involved. We not only missed her play, but her leadership, personality and the fun she brings to the team."

Shults couldn't endure the pain and the weight loss forever. In early May, she was diagnosed with ulcerative colitis, a chronic disease of the colon. On May 20, she was admitted to a hospital with malnutrition after losing 25 pounds.

Intensive medication, though, gave Shults her life back. She returned to the lineup for one game of the College World Series in 2011 and took off from there. As a senior, she was the catcher for the 2013 national champs. She set the school and Big 12 record for home runs and was a three-time All-America. She had the highest fielding percentage of any catcher in OU history.

And all with a new attitude about softball. Shults admitted her mind-set about the game had changed, that because she had lost it for the first time in her life, she returned with "a greater sense of urgency and vigor." More than anything else, she found once again the joy of playing the game she loved.

How's your attitude? You can fuss because your house is not as big as some, because a coworker talks too much, or because you have to take pills every day. Or you can appreciate your home for providing warmth and shelter, the co-worker for the lively conversation, and the medicine for keeping you reasonably healthy.

Whether life is endured or enjoyed depends largely on your attitude. An attitude of thankfulness to God offers you the best chance to get the most out of your life because living in gratitude means you choose joy no matter what your circumstances. This world does not exist to satisfy you, so chances are it will not. True contentment and joy are found in a deep, abiding relationship with God, and the proper way to approach God is not with haughtiness or anger but with gratitude for all he has given you.

I forgot how much fun it is to play this game.

-- *Jessica Shults*

**Your attitude goes a long way
toward determining the quality of your life
and of your relationship with God.**

CALLING IT QUITS

Read Numbers 13:25-14:4.

"The men who had gone up with him said, 'We can't attack those people; they are stronger than we are'" (v. 13:31).

The player whom many would consider "the finest option quarterback in OU history" had decided to quit the Sooner team. And then the Lord spoke to him.

From 1975-78, Thomas Lott led the Sooners to 23 wins in his 29 starts. He was All-Big Eight in 1977 and '78 and a team captain in '78. He accounted for more than 3,000 yards in his career.

The first black quarterback to start for the Sooners, Lott often drew as much attention for his trademark bandana as he did for his play. He had a practical reason for wearing it: to protect his Afro. Once, though, Lott asked head coach Barry Switzer if he should ditch the headpiece. "You've been wearing it ever since high school," Switzer replied. "You're wearing it so you won't have to stand around with that pick for 20 minutes."

The bandana stayed. Linebacker Daryl Hunt said Lott was like a folk hero among many of the players. "When Thomas broke out his bandana, I broke out mine," Hunt said. "Mine was like Aunt Jemima. I tied mine up in the front."

But OU fans came close to missing that bandana and the wins that came with it. At one point, Lott had decided to quit the team.

He told himself that he would be starting by the end of the

fourth game of his sophomore season. But in that fourth game, he didn't play a down. "Emotionally and mentally, I was quitting," he said. "I was mad at the world."

That Saturday night he made up his mind to leave Norman. But when he woke up Sunday morning, he was calm. "I just felt different once I woke up," he said. "I like to tell people that the Lord spoke to me that night in a dream."

Lott decided to give it one more week. He started the following game against Texas.

Remember that time you quit a high-school sports team or that night you bailed out of a relationship? That day you walked away from a job with the goals unachieved? Sometimes quitting is the most sensible way to minimize your losses, so you may well at times in your life give up on something or someone.

In your relationship with God, however, you should remember the people of Israel, who quit when the Promised Land was theirs for the taking. They forgot one fact of life you never should: God never gives up on you.

That means you should never, ever give up on God. No matter how tired or discouraged you get, no matter that it seems your prayers aren't getting through to God, no matter what – quitting on God is not an option.

He is preparing a blessing for you, and in his time, he will bring it to fruition -- if you don't quit on him.

I had been named the starter at the brink of my self-imposed deadline.
-- Thomas Lott

Whatever else you give up on in your life, don't give up on God; he will never ever give up on you.

GOOD ADVICE

Read Isaiah 8:11-9:7.

"And he will be called Wonderful Counselor" (v. 9:6b).

Roy Williams got some good advice from a coach. He promptly ignored it and pulled what has been called "maybe the single most revered play in Sooners history."

A junior in 2001, Williams, a strong safety, won the Bronko Nagurski Trophy as the nation's best defensive player and the Jim Thorpe Award as the country's best defensive back. He was a unanimous All-America selection and was the Big 12 Defensive Player of the Year.

The Red River Shootout of '01 was a battle of ranked and undefeated teams with Texas favored over the defending champs.

OU led 7-3 early in the fourth quarter when the coaches called for "Slamdog," which turned Williams loose on a blitz. He shot the gap between the left guard and tackle and attempted to hurdle the Texas blocking back. It didn't go well. He took a foot in the groin, and the Longhorn quarterback ran past him for 11 yards.

With only 2:06 to play, Texas was backed up to its own 3, and the coaches called for Slamdog again. After what had happened on the previous blitz, OU defensive coordinator Mike Stoops had some advice for his star: "Don't leave your feet!"

Williams didn't pay a lick of attention; what resulted has been dubbed "The Superman Play." He launched himself over that same blocking back and right into the UT quarterback. The collision popped the ball into the surprised but waiting arms of linebacker Teddy Lehman. He waltzed into the end zone to clinch the 14-3 Sooner win.

The play has been immortalized with a mural in OU's Roy Williams Strength and Speed Complex.

Like football players, we all need a little advice now and then. More often that not, we turn to professional counselors, who are all over the place. Marriage counselors, grief counselors, guidance counselors in our schools, rehabilitation counselors, all sorts of mental health and addiction counselors -- We even have pet counselors. No matter what our situation or problem, we can find plenty of advice for the taking.

The problem, of course, is that we find advice easy to offer but hard to swallow. We also have a rueful tendency to solicit the wrong source for advice, seeking counsel that doesn't really solve our problem but that instead enables us to continue with it.

Our need for outside advice, for an independent perspective on our situation, is actually God-given. God serves many functions in our lives, but one role clearly delineated in his Word is that of Counselor. Jesus himself is described as the "Wonderful Counselor." All the advice we need in our lives is right there for the asking; we don't even have to pay for it except with our faith. God is always there for us: to listen, to lead, and to guide.

It felt like I was in the air forever.
-- Roy Williams on leaving his feet despite his coach's advice

We all need and seek advice in our lives, but the ultimate and most Wonderful Counselor is of divine and not human origin.

TALK IT OVER

Read Luke 24:13-35.

"Then the two told what had happened on the way" (v. 35).

Steve Rhodes was basically recruited to Oklahoma by a sailor.

Rhodes was a four-year starter at wide receiver and captain of the 1980 team. In the era of the Oklahoma wishbone, he caught only 43 passes but averaged 17.3 yards per catch.

A big-time talent, Rhodes had narrowed his choices down to OU, Arkansas, and Texas A&M when he made his official visit to Norman on a foggy night in January 1975. The trip offered a big bonus for the youngster; it was his first-ever plane ride. So he excitedly boarded a plane in Dallas for a flight that was scheduled to arrive in Oklahoma City around 7 p.m. It never made it.

The fog that had been rather light in Dallas was pea soup in Oklahoma City. The flight was diverted to Wichita, Kansas.

"I'm sitting there waiting for Steve's flight to arrive," recalled Sooner assistant coach Jerry Pettibone. "Suddenly they announce it's going to Wichita instead." That set Pettibone scrambling to find someone in the Wichita airport to give Rhodes a message with his phone number on it. Rhodes got the message, and not being an expert on airplane flights, he wanted to know what the heck was going on.

The fog never did clear up, so later that night, the passengers loaded onto a bus and rode to Norman. The vehicle pulled into town around 1 a.m.

As each hour passed, Pettibone's anxiety grew. He figured they had lost the recruit because of the awful trip. To the coach's dismay and delight, however, Rhodes exited the bus laughing and talking to a U.S. sailor who had just spent the last three hours telling him how much he loved OU football and what a great place Oklahoma really was.

The talkative sailor pretty much did the job. Rhodes committed to OU a few weeks later.

Sooner fans like that sailor can't help themselves. Put two of them together and they've just got to talk about OU football, the players, the coaches, the great plays, the big wins.

A similar situation occurred way back on that first Easter when a trio of travelers was hiking down the road. One of them must not have been from around there, so two of them had to tell him all about what had been going on. Then when the two men realized their companion was the risen Lord, they went to Jerusalem to talk some more, to tell others what had happened. They found another group as excited as they were and talking about the events of the day.

So it continues today; for two millennia now, people have talked about Jesus. That's because even today, just as it was for the two men on the road to Emmaus, meeting Jesus always leaves us with something to talk about.

[The sailor] basically recruited Steve to OU for us.
-- Jerry Pettibone on Rhodes' talkative buddy on the bus ride

**An encounter with the living Jesus always
leaves us with something to talk about.**

SOONER PRIDE

Read 1 John 2:15-17.

"Everything in the world -- the desire of the flesh, the desire of the eyes, the pride in riches -- comes not from the Father but from the world" (v. 16 NRSV).

Sometimes pride and effort are all you have."

Thursday, March 11, 2004, the OU men's basketball team took on Nebraska in the opening round of the Big 12 Tournament. The first half was as horrific as any the Sooners had played all season. As the game wore on, they wound up down to nothing but pride and effort.

How bad was it? Forward Johnnie Gilbert fouled out with 8:55 to play. Center Larry Turner and guard Lawrence McKenzie had to play less aggressively for much of the last half because they each had four fouls. The two guards averaging about 11 points a game were in trouble: freshman Drew Lavender cramped up and Jason Detrick limped from a blow to the body. Former starting forward Kevin Bookout watched in street clothes, his shoulder still mending from surgery. The player who took his spot in the lineup had been booted off the team. All of this was packaged with a first half in which "the ball bounced everywhere but into the Sooners' basket." As a result, Nebraska led 35-22 at the break.

At halftime, though, OU head coach Kelvin Sampson preached his basketball gospel of "heart and sweat and scraped knees and bruised ribs and all those other Sooner basketball badges of

SOONERS

honor." It all boiled down to pride and effort because under the circumstances that was all the Sooners had left. It was enough.

"In the second half, we forgot about the shots and played hard and knew everything would take care of itself," Detrick said. It did. The Sooners rallied, the Huskers faded. Part of a 10-0 run propelled the Sooners into a 41-40 lead with 12:18 left. They won 63-59 on a night when their Sooner pride carried them to victory.

What are you most proud of? The size of your bank account? The trophies from your tennis league? The title under your name at the office? Your family?

Pride is one of life's great paradoxes. You certainly want a surgeon who takes pride in her work or a Sooner coach who is proud of his team's accomplishments. But pride in the things and the people of this world is inevitably disappointing because it leads to dependence upon things that will pass away and idolization of people who will fail you. Self-pride is even more dangerous because it inevitably leads to self-glorification.

Pride in the world's baubles and its people lures you to the earthly and the temporary, and away from God and the eternal. Pride in yourself yields the same results in that you exalt yourself and not God.

God alone is glorious enough to be worshipped. Jesus Christ alone is Lord.

A lot of players on this team do have a lot of pride.
-- Jason Detrick explaining the win over Nebraska

Pride can be dangerous because it tempts you to lower your sight from God and the eternal to the world and the temporary.

DAY 50

BAD IDEA

Read Mark 14:43-50.

"The betrayer had arranged a signal with them: 'The one I kiss is the man; arrest him and lead him away under guard'" (v. 44).

It sounded like a good idea: Get this explosive runner more involved in the offense by moving him to wide receiver, thus getting him off the bench. Bad idea.

In the 62-21 rout of Missouri in the 2008 Big 12 championship game, sophomore running back Mossis Madu exploded onto the scene. Seeming to come out of nowhere, he rushed for 114 yards and scored three touchdowns. The Sooners quite obviously had a player on their hands they needed to do more with.

So the coaches came up with what seemed like a pretty good idea at the time: Let's move this guy to wide receiver so we can get the ball to him more often. The experiment failed.

"Last year (2009) was a big disaster," Madu said. It just didn't work out. After a sophomore season in which he rushed for 475 yards, had 11 receptions, and scored six touchdowns, Madu had only five carries for 17 yards and seven receptions and no touchdowns his junior season. He struggled with the new position and only rarely even made it onto the field.

Madu did manage to find something good about the bad idea. "It was a learning process for me," he said about the long season. "[It] taught me how to work even harder for what I want."

SOONERS

It helped that during the off-season the coaches came up with what Madu really regarded as a good idea: They moved him back to running back for 2010. He was stuck as the backup to DeMarco Murray, but he was much more productive. And much happier. "I'm loving it," he said. "[I'm] just trying to go out and have fun."

The combination of Murray and Madu worked so well that he received a game ball after the 28-20 win over Texas. The pairing worked all season as the Sooners went 12-2 and won the Big 12.

That sure-fire investment you made from a pal's hot stock tip. The expensive exercise machine that now traps dust bunnies under your bed. Blond hair. Telling your wife you wanted to eat at the restaurant with the waitresses in the skimpy shorts. They seemed like pretty good ideas at the time; they weren't.

We all have bad ideas in our lifetime. They provide some of our most crucial learning experiences. Even the OU coaches learned from the failed experiment with Mossis Madu at receiver.

Some ideas, though, are so irreparably and inherently bad that we cannot help but wonder why they were even conceived in the first place. Almost two thousand years ago a man had just such an idea. Judas' betrayal of Jesus remains to this day one of the most heinous acts of treachery in history.

Turning his back on Jesus was a bad idea for Judas then; it's a bad idea for us now.

When he is in there, you feel good about it.
— Bob Stoops on the good idea of Mossis Madu at running back

We all have some pretty bad ideas
during our lifetime, but nothing equals
the folly of turning away from Jesus.

DAY 51

REST EASY

Read Hebrews 4:1-11.

*"There remains, then, a Sabbath rest for the people of God;
for anyone who enters God's rest also rests from his own
work, just as God did from his. Let us, therefore, make
every effort to enter that rest" (vv. 9-11).*

Six weeks of bed rest is an awful sentence for an athletic boy.
At least Jack Mitchell got a high school sweetheart out of the deal.

As a senior in 1948, Mitchell was named OU's first All-American
quarterback. He may well have been the originator of the quarterback option, though history credits a Missouri head coach
with that innovation in 1941. Mitchell still holds the major-college
career record for average yards gained per punt return at 23.6.

He was the first sophomore in the history of his high school to
make the varsity football team, but he also contracted rheumatic
fever that year and wound up with a faulty heart valve. A doctor
said the boy could be healthy and fully active again if his heart
valve completely closed . The only way to entice that reaction was
complete bed rest for at least six weeks. So young Jack Mitchell
went to bed.

Really to bed. "I couldn't even get up to go to the bathroom or
to eat," he recalled. "I guess if you tie a horse up to a post long
enough, the horse gets used to it. So I got used to it." He listened
to the radio quite a bit, his friends brought him books, and his
mother had a teacher drop by to keep him from getting behind

in school.

Mitchell also became something of a celebrity as the local kids dropped by to see this weird sight of a kid in bed all the time. For Mitchell, the best part was that the girls "would give me a kiss -- and on the lips, too, not one of those cheek kisses." One particular girl came with a bunch of her friends one day, and when Mitchell left his bed behind, she was the first one he asked for a date. She became his sweetheart through high school.

As part of the natural rhythm of life, rest is important to maintain physical health even if it doesn't involve spending six weeks in bed. Rest has different images, though: a good eight hours in the sack; a Saturday morning in the backyard that begins with the paper and a pot of coffee; a vacation in the mountains, where the most strenuous thing you do is change position in the hot tub.

Rest is also part of the rhythm and the health of our spiritual lives. Often we envision the faithful person as always busy and, always doing something for God whether it's teaching Sunday school or showing up at church every time the doors open.

But God himself rested from work, and in blessing us with the Sabbath, he calls us into a time of rest. To rest by simply spending time in the presence of God is to receive spiritual revitalization and rejuvenation. Sleep refreshes your body and your mind; God's rest refreshes your soul.

It kind of got to be a thing for the local kids to come by and see me in bed, like I was a circus act or something.
                                        -- Jack Mitchell on his extended bed rest

**God promises you a spiritual rest
that renews and refreshes your soul.**

CHANGES

Read Romans 6:1-14.

"Just as Christ was raised from the dead through the glory of the Father, we too may live a new life" (v. 4).

Since the season was under way, it was not exactly the ideal time to make a radical change. It turned out all right, though.

Even though Steve Owens won the Heisman Trophy in 1969, the Sooners managed only a 6-4 record. The heat was on head coach Chuck Fairbanks to the extent that then-offensive coordinator Barry Switzer felt the 28-27 win over Oklahoma State at season's end may have saved the staff's jobs.

The coaches needed to turn things around immediately, so they installed the veer offense in 1970. They hoped the switch from the I-formation would give junior quarterback Jack Mildren the freedom to direct a dynamic offense.

The change didn't work. In the first three games, the Sooners couldn't sustain drives. Switzer said the veer "was hit and miss." After a stunning loss to Oregon State that left the team 2-1, the coaches were convinced they had to make another change.

Switzer had previously talked to Fairbanks about the offense Texas was running, this thing called the wishbone. "They were running all over the yard and no one could stop them," Switzer said. "It was pretty clear we had better athletes than Texas did, so why not switch to the wishbone?"

The coaches decided to change the offense again, a decision

that has been called "the most significant and gutsy move in OU's football history." The Oklahoma wishbone was unveiled two weeks later in a loss to Texas, but the change saved the coaches' jobs and "made possible Oklahoma's second football dynasty."

With the wishbone over the next twenty seasons, Oklahoma won three national titles, had win streaks of twenty-eight and twenty games, and led the nation in rushing eight times.

The timing was horrible, but the change was one for the better.

Anyone who asserts no change is needed in his or her life just isn't paying attention. Every life has doubt, worry, fear, failure, frustration, unfulfilled dreams, and unsuccessful relationships in some combination. The memory and consequences of our past often haunt and trouble us.

Simply recognizing the need for change in our lives, though, doesn't mean the changes that will bring about hope, joy, peace, and fulfillment will occur. We need some power greater than ourselves or we wouldn't be where we are.

So where can we turn to? Where lies the hope for a changed life? It lies in an encounter with the Lord of all Hope: Jesus Christ. For a life turned over to Jesus, change is inevitable. With Jesus in charge, the old self with its painful and destructive ways of thinking, feeling, loving, and living is transformed.

A changed life is always only a talk with Jesus away.

To change in the middle of the season, that's a terrifically tough decision. I found it hard to fathom why.
-- Jack Mildren on his reaction to the change to the wishbone

**In Jesus lie the hope and the power
that change lives.**

DAY 53

JUST PERFECT

Read Matthew 5:43-48.

"Be perfect, therefore, as your heavenly Father is perfect"
(v. 48).

Perfection may not exist in football, but the Sooners once came so close that the contest was dubbed "The Perfect Game."

Just how perfect was the 77-0 slaughter of Texas A&M on Nov. 8, 2003? Well, the only participants wearing an Aggie uniform to cross midfield that day were the members of the band, and the Sooner defense did not allow a third-down conversion the entire game. The Aggies were 0-for-12.

The score may not indicate it, but the Sooners even managed perfectly to avoid running up the score -- somewhat. "We didn't want to get to 80," said offensive coordinator Chuck Long. "That's not what we wanted to do." Befitting perfection, they didn't.

"You don't expect this," declared head coach Bob Stoops. The Sooners were ranked No. 1 in the nation, and the Aggies were having a down year, but they still went into the game at 4-5. They simply ran into the gridiron equivalent of virtual perfection. OU rolled up 639 yards while holding A&M to a grand total of 54 yards and only three first downs.

The game was a blowout by halftime. The Sooners scored on seven of their eight possessions before the break and led 49-0. Heisman-Trophy winner Jason White completed his first fourteen passes and wound up tossing five TD passes.

SOONERS

The score ran to 77-0 with more than a quarter to play. The game ended with a handoff to a walk-on fullback on a play that wasn't even in the playbook. With 8:18 left, OU took a knee near the A&M goal line, then ran three plays at half-speed.

Oklahoma "is definitely the best team in the nation," declared A&M offensive tackle Alan Reuber. On this particular day, OU was also the closest thing the nation would see to a perfect team.

Nobody's perfect; we all make mistakes every day. We botch our personal relationships; at work we seek competence, not perfection. To insist upon personal or professional perfection in our lives is to establish an impossibly high standard that will eventually destroy us physically, emotionally, and mentally.

Yet that is exactly the standard God sets for us. Our love is to be perfect, never ceasing, never failing, never qualified – just the way God loves us. And Jesus didn't limit his command to only preachers and goody-two-shoes types. All of his disciples are to be perfect as they navigate their way through the world's ambiguous definition and understanding of love.

But that's impossible! Well, not necessarily, if to love perfectly is to serve God wholeheartedly and to follow Jesus with single-minded devotion. Anyhow, in his perfect love for us, God makes allowance for our imperfect love and the consequences of it in the perfection of Jesus.

If we chase perfection, we can catch excellence.

-- Vince Lombardi

**In his perfect love for us, God provides a way
for us to escape the consequences
of our imperfect love for him: Jesus.**

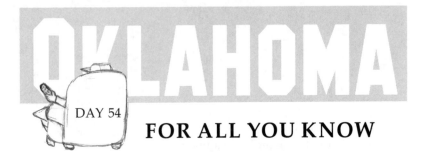

FOR ALL YOU KNOW

Read John 8:12-32.

"You will know the truth, and the truth will set you free"
(v. 32).

Jelena Cerina completed her college basketball career as a Sooner in 2011-12. Yet, as her time in high school wound down, she didn't even know where the University of Oklahoma was.

Despite being a star in high school, Cerina had no plans to play college ball. Her situation wasn't unique where she was, though; that would be Serbia. "A lot of players overseas, after high school, just play basketball," she said. "They don't go to college." So Cerina didn't know much of anything about college basketball in the States, let alone in Oklahoma.

That changed, though, when she landed a spot on the Serbian women's national team. Her more informed teammates talked freely about playing on a scholarship at junior colleges in America. That intrigued Cerina.

Still, she didn't know how to go about getting to an American college. Then a junior college coach saw her play and dropped her an e-mail asking if she'd ever considered playing junior college ball in the United States. Fortunately for the Sooners, the school was Northeastern Oklahoma A&M. "Literally in May, I was like, 'I want to do this,'" Cerina said. "And in August I was at NEO."

She traveled halfway around the world to Miami, OK, without ever having seen the campus, relying on the coach's assertion that it would be a good place for her. The coach was right; Cerina flourished in this brand new world. After her sophomore season, OU was among the schools that came calling. "I never imagined I'd be playing for OU. It's incredible," she said.

In her senior season of 2011-12, Cerina played in every game, a reserve center who averaged just under four points and four rebounds per game. The adventure that took her to a place she knew virtually nothing about was more than she had ever dreamed.

Like Jelena Cerina and her limited knowledge of the opportunities available in American basketball, there's much you just flat don't know. Maybe it's the formula for the area of a cylinder or the capital of Myanmar. You may not know how paper is made from trees. Or how toothpaste gets into the tube. And can you honestly say you know how the opposite sex thinks?

Despite your ignorance about certain subjects, you manage quite well because what you don't know generally doesn't hurt you too much. In certain aspects of your life, though, ignorance is anything but harmless. Imagine, for instance, the consequence of not knowing how to do your job. Or of getting behind the wheel without knowing how to drive a car.

In your faith life, what you don't know can have awful, eternal consequences. To willfully choose not to know Jesus is to be condemned to an eternity apart from God. When it comes to Jesus, knowing the truth sets you free; ignoring the truth enslaves you.

We never heard anything about colleges.
— Jelena Cerina on not knowing about American college ball

What you don't know may not hurt you
except when it comes to Jesus.

JUGGERNAUT

Read Revelation 20.

"Fire came down from heaven and devoured them. And the devil, who deceived them, was thrown into the lake of burning sulfur, where the beast and the false prophet had been thrown" (vv. 9b-10a).

Sports *Illustrated* finally declared what those luckless enough to play the 2008 Sooners already knew: They were a juggernaut.

SI's official proclamation came after Oklahoma pummeled Missouri 62-21 in the Big 12 championship game. Sophomore quarterback Sam Bradford, who won the Heisman Trophy, was so good that season that when he threw for 384 yards on 34-of-49 passing against Missouri, his quarterback rating *dropped*. Nevertheless, it remained higher than the ten quarterbacks before him who had won college football's biggest prize.

Bradford was the leader of the greatest offensive juggernaut in college football history. The team set a major division record in the modern era by scoring 702 points. They were the first team in 89 seasons to score 60 or more points in five straight games. They scored more than 50 points in four other games.

Just how good was this offense? If a statistician counted only the points the Sooners scored in the first half all season, they would still be the 18th-highest scoring team in the country.

While Bradford's season of 48 touchdown passes and only six interceptions was not the stuff of mortals, sportswriter Albert

SOONERS

Chen noted that "what has turned Oklahoma into a juggernaut is its evolving ground game." With Chris Brown's 1,110 yards rushing and another 1,002 yards from sophomore DeMarco Murray, OU was the first team in major college history to have a 4,000-yard passer and two 1,000-yard rushers.

The only thing that had trouble moving against Missouri in the championship game was the Sooner Schooner, which broke down after Oklahoma's first touchdown. Appropriately, it was soon up and running again at full speed.

Maybe your experience with a juggernaut involved a football or basketball game against a team chock full of major college prospects, a league tennis match against a former college player, or your presentation for the project you knew didn't stand a chance. Whatever it was, you've been slam-dunked before.

Being part of a juggernaut is certainly more fun than being in the way of one. Just ask OU's opponents in 2008. Or consider the forces of evil aligned against God. At least the teams that took the field against OU in 2008 had some hope, however slim, that they might win. No such hope exists for those who oppose God.

That's because their fate is already spelled out in detail. It's in the book; we all know how the story ends. God's enemies may talk big and bluster now, but they will be soundly trounced and routed in the most decisive defeat of all time.

You sure want to be on the winning side in that one.

I'd never been to a mercy killing before.
-- Basketball coach Benny Dees after a 101-76 loss

The most lopsided victory in all of history is a sure thing: God's ultimate triumph over evil.

DAY 56

HOMELESS

Read Matthew 8:18-22.

"Jesus replied, 'Foxes have holes and birds of the air have nests, but the Son of Man has no place to lay his head'" (v. 20).

From homeless to the Heisman. That's the journey of OU's Billy Vessels.

When Vessels was 14, his parents and his older brother moved to Oklahoma City from Cleveland. Young Billy simply refused to go, so he was left behind.

He was homeless. He bounced from family to family and did odd jobs around town to earn spending money. With some of the townspeople paying his bills, Vessels said in later years that the town raised him. The local newspaper publisher eventually took the youngster under his wing and began taking him to some OU football games. When he met Bud Wilkinson, Vessels decided to play for the Sooners.

He arrived in Norman in 1949 and became a starter as a sophomore, leading the Sooners in 1950 to their first national title. In the second game of the 1951 season, though, Vessels injured a knee and missed the remainder of the season.

He adopted an unusual method of rehabbing the knee, spending the summer of 1952 running barefoot along the banks of the Arkansas River. He ran for miles each day in the hot, dry river sand, building up his knee.

SOONERS

It held up very nicely as Vessels rushed for 1,072 yards and scored 17 touchdowns for the 8-1-1 Sooners. For all purposes, he clinched the Heisman Trophy in the team's only loss. With the whole country watching the first football game to be televised nationally, Vessels rushed for 195 yards and scored three touchdowns in a tough 27-21 loss to the Irish.

The once-homeless boy was the toast of New York and his home state, the first Sooner to win the Heisman Trophy.

Rock bottom in America has a face: the bag lady pushing a shopping cart; the scruffy guy with a beard and a backpack at the interstate exit holding a cardboard sign. Look closer at that bag lady or that scruffy guy, though, and you may see desperate women with children fleeing violence, veterans haunted by their combat experiences, or sick or injured workers.

Few of us are indifferent to the homeless when we're around them. They often raise quite strong passions, whether we regard them as a ministry or an odorous nuisance. They trouble us, perhaps because we realize that we're only one catastrophic illness and a few paychecks away from joining them. They remind us of how tenuous our own holds upon material success really are.

But they also stir our compassion because we serve a Lord who – like them -- had no home, and for whom, the homeless, too, are his children.

Some people beat up on the homeless for sport.
-- Maryland State Sen. Lisa Gladden

**Because they, too, are God's children,
the homeless merit our compassion, not our scorn.**

STORY TIME

Read Luke 8:26-39.

"'Return home and tell how much God has done for you.'
So the man went away and told all over town how much
Jesus had done for him" (v. 39).

Sand burrs. No pads. An amputation. A deaf referee. Oh, the Sooners of 1907 could tell some stories.

Football was catching on in Norman by 1907, but that didn't mean the game was exactly the often seamless operation we are used to today. When the Sooners beat Epworth University 29-0 in a game played in Oklahoma City, the field was full of sand burrs. That meant the ball was, too. Captain and quarterback Bill Cross took charge; he was the only one willing to handle the ball. "That was one game I had all the indirect passes I wanted," he said.

The squad played three games in seven days. In the loss to A&M, an OU player had a tooth driven through his lower lip; he didn't miss a play. Against Texas, legendary coach Bennie Owen, normally mild-mannered, was upset enough to protest to an official, who didn't seem to care about anything the coach said. Only later did Owen learn that the referee was a coach from the nearby Texas School for the Deaf and couldn't hear a thing.

Tragedy struck Owen three days before the season began. As he was loading up after a day spent quail hunting, his shotgun accidentally discharged, sending pellets into his right arm and severing an artery. The arm was amputated. Visitors found the coach more concerned about the start of the season than the loss of his arm. He was back on the practice field within days.

Newcomer Charley Wantland reported to his first practice that season carrying his football helmet. He quickly noticed, though, that the other players were bare-headed, so he stashed the helmet in a hedge and "joined the head-banging fearlessly." "Owen believed in conditioning, not protective equipment" and disdained gear such as helmets because it slowed his players down.

Yep, the Sooners of '07 had a story or two to tell.

You, too, have a story to tell; it's the story of your life and it's unique. No one else among the billions of people on this planet can tell the same story.

Part of that story is your encounter with Jesus. It's the most important chapter of all, but, strangely enough, believers in Jesus Christ often don't tell it. Otherwise brave and daring Christian men and women who wouldn't think twice of skydiving or white-water rafting often quail when we are faced with the prospect of speaking about Jesus to someone else. It's the dreaded "W" word: witness. "I just don't know what to say," we sputter.

But witnessing is nothing but telling your story. No one can refute it; no one can claim it isn't true. You don't get into some great theological debate for which you're ill prepared. You just tell the beautiful, awesome story of Jesus and you.

To succeed in your sport or your life, you have to go out and write your own story.
-- *Motivational-Quotes-for-Athletes.com*

We all have a story to tell, but the most important part of all is the chapter where we meet Jesus.

REDEEMED

Read 1 Peter 1:17-25.

"It was not with perishable things such as silver or gold that you were redeemed from the empty way of life handed down to you from your forefathers, but with the precious blood of Christ" (vv. 18-19).

David Godbold was so deep in his coach's doghouse that he needed some redemption. A game-winning shot took care of that.

A 6-5 guard from Oklahoma City, Godbold played in 123 games over his four seasons from 2004-2008. Against Texas Tech on Feb. 16, 2008, though, he was on the bench, his starting spot handed over to freshman Tony Neysmith. There was a good reason for it.

Godbold had angered head coach Jeff Capel and the entire OU staff a week earlier in a disappointing 14-point loss to Colorado. He had dribbled out the final 15 seconds while squatting near midcourt. Capel never said Godbold's actions against Colorado were behind his benching for the Tech game. The head Sooner was clear, however, that he was upset, saying during the week that the situation would be handled within the program.

Though he didn't start, Godbold was on the court when his team needed him the most. With 10 seconds left to play, Tech led 64-63. Capel drew up a play for point guard Austin Johnson, who nailed six 3-pointers and had a career-high 20 points. Tech was ready for him, though, and he couldn't get an open shot. He was forced to drop the ball off to Godbold, who let fly with a 28-foot bomb as soon as he touched it. He hit nothing but net with 1.4 seconds left; Oklahoma had a big 66-64 win, and Godbold had his redemption.

"Hopefully it propels us to another level," Godbold said about the win with his eyes on the NCAA Tournament. It did just that. The defeat of Tech upped the Sooners to the crucial .500 level in conference play. They finished the season 23-12 and advanced to the second round of the NCAA Tournament.

In our capitalistic society, we know all about redemption. Just think "rebate" or store or product coupons. To receive the rebates or the discount, though, we must redeem them, cash them in.

"Redemption" is a business term; it reconciles a debt, restoring one party to favor by making amends as was the case with David Godbold and head coach Jeff Capel. In the Bible, a slave could obtain his freedom only upon the paying of money by a redeemer. In other words, redemption involves the cancelling of a debt the individual cannot pay on his own.

While literal, physical slavery is incomprehensible to us today, we nevertheless live much like slaves in our relationship to sin. On our own, we cannot escape from its consequence, which is death. We need a redeemer, someone to pay the debt that gives us the forgiveness from sin we cannot give ourselves.

We have such a redeemer. He is Jesus Christ, who paid our debt not with money, but with his own blood.

The doghouse is where you sit on the end of the bench and don't play.
-- David Godbold, asserting his benching was to motivate him

To accept Jesus Christ as your savior is to believe that his death was a selfless act of redemption.

THOSE THINGS

Read Luke 13:1-9.

"Do you think they were more guilty than all the others living in Jerusalem? I tell you, no!" (vv 4b, 5a)

Bad breaks are part of any football game. In the 1985 Orange Bowl, though, the Sooners got one of the strangest bad breaks of all time: The mascot drew a penalty.

With the game against Washington tied at 14 early in the fourth quarter, the Sooners lined up for a go-ahead field goal, a 22-yard chip shot for OU kicker Tim Lashar. But an OU lineman who had been checking in and out of the game wearing jerseys 79 and 90 neglected to notify the official this time. Lashar's kick was good, but the refs flagged the Sooners for an illegal substitution.

As soon as Lashar's kick sailed through the uprights and the ref's arms went up, the Sooner Schooner swung into action. Speed was important so the game wouldn't be delayed. Proper procedure was followed that included checking the field for a flag. The starter didn't see one, and everything went off without a hitch.

Until the Schooner got onto the field. The driver realized something was wrong when he saw the officials huddling on the far side of the field. He turned the ponies to get back to the sideline, but they were on unfamiliar turf and were running in the opposite direction they were accustomed to. "They actually kind of froze up and stopped," the driver said.

Because of the high crown on the field, the starter hadn't been able to see the flag. The driver turned the ponies and drove the Schooner toward the end zone, but a referee threw a flag for a 15-yard unsportsmanlike conduct penalty.

This time, the Huskies blocked the more formidable 42-yard kick. "The wheels pretty much came off for us after that," Lashar said, and Washington won the game.

A penalty on the Sooner Schooner was just one of those things.

You've probably had a few of "those things" in your own life: bad breaks that occur without regard to justice, morality, or fair play. You wonder if everything in life is random with events determined by a chance roll of some cosmic dice. Is there really somebody scripting all this with logic and purpose?

Yes, there is; God is the author of everything.

We know how it all began; we even know how it all will end. It's in God's book. The part we play in God's kingdom, though, is in the middle, and that part is still being revealed. The simple truth is that God's ways are different from ours. That's why we don't know what's coming our way, and why "those things" -- such as a tower falling on bystanders or our team's mascot drawing a penalty -- catch us by surprise and dismay us when they do occur.

What God asks of us is that we trust him. As the one – and the only one – in charge, he knows everything will be all right for those who follow Jesus.

The whole thing was just strange, the way it all played out.
-- OU kicker Tim Lashar on the penalty on the Schooner

Life confounds us because, while we know the end and the beginning of God's great story, we are part of the middle, which God is still writing.

RAISING A STINK

Read John 11:1-16, 38-44.

"'But, Lord,' said Martha, the sister of the dead man, 'by this time there is a bad odor, for he has been there four days.' Then Jesus said, 'Did I not tell you that if you believed, you would see the glory of God?'" (vv. 39-40)

For a while when he was at Oklahoma, Wahoo McDaniel kinda smelled bad. It had nothing to with normal body odor either.

Ed McDaniel's nickname came from his father, who was known as "Big Wahoo." He was part Chickasaw and part Choctaw and thus derived his persona of an American Indian in his pro wrestling career, the part of his life for which he is most famous.

A natural at whatever sport he tried, McDaniel starred at fullback in high school. He wanted to play college football for the best, and that meant Oklahoma in 1956. He and head coach Bud Wilkinson, a strict disciplinarian, had their differences, primarily involving the observance of team rules.

In Norman, McDaniel was moved to defensive and offensive end. He lettered three times (1957-59) and still holds the record for the longest OU punt ever: 91 yards in 1958.

As good as he was on the football field, though, McDaniel was perhaps as legendary for his exploits off the field. He just would not turn down a wager, no matter how outlandish it was.

For instance, he won $185 when some fellow athletes bet him he couldn't run the thirty-six miles form the dorm steps to the city limits of Chickasha without stopping. "It was brutal," McDaniel said about his six-hour run. But he made it.

He also once ate a gallon of jalapeno peppers on a bet.

One wager he didn't win, though, involved drinking a quart of motor oil. McDaniel gave it a try, but stopped after a few tablespoons. "That oil made me sick," he said. "For months every time I'd sweat, I could feel the stuff oozing out. I smelled like an old pickup truck."

It's a smelly world we live in. Grease traps, full garbage cans on a summer day, dirty sneakers, rotten meat -- they stink. It's also an aromatic world we live in. Roses, coffee percolating, freshly laundered clothes, your loved one's body spray -- they intoxicate.

Nothing, however, stinks both literally and metaphorically as does death. Literally: Think road kill. Metaphorically: Think life's end. We get both in the account of Jesus' raising of Lazarus from the dead. It's a tableau right out of a Christian-themed horror house with Martha's concern about the smell and the image of Lazarus stumbling out of the grave wrapped in his burial cloths.

But it's a glorious story that soars far beyond a trite Halloween scenario. In it, Jesus reveals himself to be the Lord of death as well as life. Death no longer stinks to high heaven but instead becomes the pathway to high heaven. Under Jesus' dominion, death itself becomes a sweet fragrance indeed.

Forget about sports as a profession. Sports make ya grunt and smell. See, be a thinker, not a stinker.
-- *Apollo Creed in* Rocky

**Because of Jesus, rather than stinking
to high heaven, death is the way to high heaven.**

MAKE NO MISTAKE

Read Mark 14:66-72.

"Then Peter remembered the word Jesus had spoken to him: 'Before the rooster crows twice you will disown me three times.' And he broke down and wept" (v. 72).

The Pride of Oklahoma Marching Band was already on the field for its halftime show. The Oklahoma State coaches, however, had made what turned out to be a costly mistake.

Gary Gibbs took over the OU football program in 1989 under a set of rather inauspicious circumstances. The NCAA had hit the Sooners with reduced scholarships, a ban on television and bowl appearances, and the loss of a recruiter. OU played Nebraska that year with fewer than fifty scholarship athletes available.

Nevertheless, the Sooners went 7-4 in '89 and sailed into Stillwater in 1990 with a flashy 4-0 record that included easy defeats of UCLA, Kansas, and Pittsburgh. The game marked the debut of freshman quarterback Cale Gundy, who set many of the Sooners' single-game, single-season, and career passing records until they were rewritten by Josh Heupel (1999-2000), Jason White (2000-04), Sam Bradford (2007-09), and Landry Jones (2009-12). The game also saw one of the most unlikely touchdowns in Oklahoma history.

With Oklahoma trailing 14-7 late in the first half, Gibbs inserted Gundy to take advantage of his passing ability. Time ran out, however, with the Sooners at their own 48. The Pride of Oklahoma dutifully began taking the field for the halftime show.

SOONERS

But the refs ruled that the State head coach had called a time out, apparently believing the Sooners would punt. Handed a gift play, Gibbs had no such intentions. He called for a Hail Mary, and Gundy launched a bomb to tight end Adrian Cooper. He hauled it in for a touchdown as the half ended for a second time.

That crucial Cowboy mistake made it a 14-14 game and completely took all of OSU's momentum away. Oklahoma won 31-17.

It's distressing but it's true: Like football teams and Simon Peter, we all make mistakes. Only one perfect man ever walked on this earth, and no one of us is he. Some mistakes are just dumb. Like locking yourself out of your car or falling into a swimming pool with your clothes on.

Other mistakes are more significant. Like heading down a path to addiction. Committing a crime. Walking out on a spouse and the children.

All these mistakes, however, from the momentarily annoying to the life-altering tragic, share one aspect: They can all be forgiven in Christ. Other folks may not forgive us; we may not even forgive ourselves. But God will forgive us when we call upon him in Jesus' name.

Thus, the twofold fatal mistake we can make is ignoring the fact that we will die one day and then subsequently ignoring the fact that Jesus is the only way to shun Hell and enter Heaven. We absolutely must get this one right.

The best coach is the one who makes the fewest mistakes.
-- *Bud Wilkinson*

**Only one mistake we make sends us to Hell
when we die: ignoring Jesus while we live.**

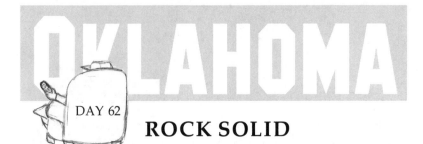

ROCK SOLID

Read Luke 6:46-49.

"I will show you what he is like who comes to me and hears my words and puts them into practice. He is like a man building a house, who dug down deep and laid the foundation on rock" (vv. 47-48).

The foundation for decades of Sooner excellence on the football field was laid by a coach who was looking for another job before he finished his first season in Norman.

Jim Tatum has been described as "one of the most interesting, colorful, effective football coaches in Oklahoma's storied history." Hired in the winter of 1946, he immediately hit the road, touring the state and "talking up Sooner football, pressing the flesh, [and] eyeing potential recruits."

Spring practice in 1946 "was like nothing anyone had ever witnessed." Potential players poured onto campus after being discharged from the military. "I never saw so many college football players in my life," said Sooner tackle Leon Manley. "They were swarming in and out carrying suitcases."

There were so many players that they filled three separate football fields. The coaches didn't know them all, so they carried note pads around. When a prospect would make a play, they would stop practice, ask his name, and scribble it down.

The result was a talented young Sooner squad that went 8-3 and finished the season strong. The team won seven of its last eight games, finishing with a 73-12 slaughter of Oklahoma State and a 34-13 thumping of NC State in the Gator Bowl.

But the season wasn't even over before Tatum let it be known he was not happy, grousing about being underpaid and deserving a longer contract. Before the bowl game, word got out that Tatum planned to interview for the Maryland job. He ultimately took it.

What Tatum left behind was a foundation for greatness: "an atmosphere of enthusiasm and an inventory of young talent." He also left behind a quite capable assistant named Bud Wilkinson.

Like OU's athletics program, your life is an ongoing project, a work in progress. As with any complex construction job, if your life is to be stable, it must have a solid foundation, which holds everything up and keeps everything together.

R. Alan Culpepper said in *The New Interpreter's Bible,* "We do not choose whether we will face severe storms in life; we only get to choose the foundation on which we will stand." In other words, tough times are inevitable. If your foundation isn't rock-solid, you will have nothing on which to stand as those storms buffet you, nothing to keep your life from flying apart into a cycle of disappointment and destruction.

But when the foundation is solid and sure, you can take the blows, stand strong, recover, and live with joy and hope. Only one foundation is sure and foolproof: Jesus Christ. Everything else you build upon will fail you.

Jesus Christ is the rock upon which I stand.
-- Heisman Trophy winner Danny Wuerffel

Your life must have its foundation in Jesus Christ,
or the first sign of trouble will knock you down.

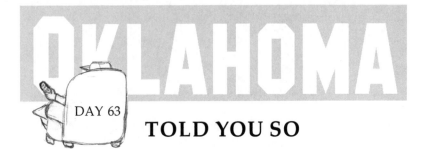

TOLD YOU SO

Read Matthew 24:15-31.

"See, I have told you ahead of time" (v. 25).

You just wait and see." That was George Cumby's reaction when they told him he wasn't good enough.

Cumby actually played in a varsity football game when he was in the fifth grade. His high school had one team that covered all the grades, and he got into the last play of the last game of the season. He carried the ball and was stuffed at the line of scrimmage. "The only thing I can remember is being upside down in the pile and I couldn't breathe," he recalled. "I couldn't wait for all of those older, bigger guys to get off of me so I could breathe again."

Cumby attended a private Catholic school in Tyler his senior season and was the fullback in a wishbone offense. He planned to go to Henderson County Junior College after graduation, which was where his brother had gone to school.

One day, though, he was summoned to the principal's office where OU assistant coach Wendell Mosley was waiting for him. One recruiting trip later, Oklahoma offered Cumby a scholarship, but he wasn't sure he would accept it. "I just didn't think I was good enough," he explained.

Cumby wasn't the only ones who had doubts. A school super-intendent told him bluntly, "You'll never make it up there." An uncle had told him the same thing. "I was determined after that," Cumby said. "My whole mind set was to prove them wrong."

He arrived at Norman in the fall of 1976, and "it was hard, very hard, once we started three-a-day practices." Cumby admitted that quitting crossed his mind, but he was determined not to fail. He wanted one day to say to that superintendent and to his uncle, "I told you so."

He did just that. Cumby was a two-time All-American linebacker who was twice the Big Eight Defensive Player of the Year. He played eight seasons in the NFL.

Don't you just hate it in when somebody says, "I told you so"? That means the other person was right and you were wrong; that other person has spoken the truth. You could have listened to that know-it-all in the first place, but then you would have lost the chance yourself to crow, "I told you so."

In our pluralistic age and society, many view truth as relative, meaning absolute truth does not exist. All belief systems have equal value and merit. But this is a ghastly, dangerous fallacy because it ignores the truth that God proclaimed in the presence and words of Jesus.

In speaking the truth, Jesus told everybody exactly what he was going to do: come back and take his faithful followers with him. Those who don't listen or who don't believe will be left behind with those four awful words, "I told you so," ringing in their ears and wringing their souls.

There was no way I was going to give up and quit after what that superintendent had told me.
> *-- George Cumby on toughing it out at OU*

**Jesus matter-of-factly told us what he has planned:
He will return to gather all the faithful to himself.**

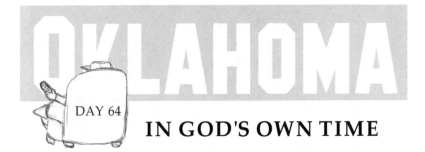

IN GOD'S OWN TIME

Read James 5:7-12.

"Be patient, then, brothers, until the Lord's coming" (v. 7).

Michael Rocha had finally exhausted his coach's patience. Only then did he begin a remarkable turnaround that left him in the OU record books.

When the Oklahoma baseball team boarded the bus to Texas Tech for a three-game series in mid-April 2010, to Rocha's shock, he was left behind. He wasn't injured; he wasn't sick. He just wasn't in head coach Sunny Golloway's plans anymore.

At the time, the junior's record wasn't that bad; he was 4-1. But he hadn't really pitched that well; his ERA was a sky-high 6.12. The weekend before, Rocha had left Golloway livid when he had grooved a pitch on an 0-2 count that a Missouri player blasted for a game-winning home run. As a result, for the first time in his career, Rocha didn't travel with the team.

"That weekend was rough," he admitted. "I was on the computer the whole time, checking the score every inning. . . . None of my roommates are there, because they're playing. None of my friends are in town, because I don't really have any outside the baseball team."

Rocha realized he had finally tested his coach's patience to its limits. "I'd been the guy, for really my first three years, who would mess up and always get that extra chance." Now Rocha wondered if he would get that extra chance one more time.

Nine days later, he did. Golloway brought him into a close game against TCU with a runner on third base and no outs. The run didn't score. That began a turnaround that culminated in Rocha's starting OU's first game of the 2010 College World Series. It continued in 2011. Rocha was chosen a team captain, went 10-3, and was All-Big 12 first team and second team All-America. He ended his OU career with 27 wins, third most in school history.

Have you ever left a restaurant because the server didn't take your order quickly enough? Complained at your doctor's office about how long you had to wait? Wondered how much longer a sermon was going to last?

It isn't just the machinations of the world with which we're impatient; we want God to move at our pace, not his. For instance, how often have you prayed and expected – indeed, demanded – an immediate answer from God? And aren't Christians the world over impatient for the glorious day when Jesus will return and set everything right? We're in a hurry but God obviously isn't.

As rare as it seems to be, patience is nevertheless included among the likes of gentleness, humility, kindness, and compassion as attributes of a Christian.

God expects us to be patient. He knows what he's doing, he is in control, and his will shall be done. On his schedule, not ours.

It was like, 'Maybe this time I finally did it. I finally pushed him to where he's not going to play me anymore.'
-- *Michael Rocha on testing coach Sunny Golloway's patience*

God moves in his own time, so often we must wait for him to act, remaining faithful and patient.

POP THE QUESTION

Read Matthew 16:13-17.

"'But what about you?' he asked. 'Who do you say I am?'" (v. 15)

Sooner offensive tackle Scott Kempenich looked up at the scoreboard and asked the question even the most casual college football fan could well ask that day: "Dang! What's up with that?"

Kempenich's calm pause among the downright delirium that was taking place all around him came at the conclusion of the 2000 Red River Shootout. This was to be another classic, a battle of ranked teams -- OU was 10th, UT 11th -- that would be hotly contested right to the finish.

Then the teams kicked off and what happened was, as junior All-American linebacker Rocky Calmus put it mildly, "more than what I expected." The Sooners piled up the most points and the most yards they had ever gained against Texas and slaughtered the Horns 63-14.

Sophomore running back Quentin Griffin set a school record with six rushing touchdowns of 1, 2, 4, 3, 8, and 1 yards. QB Josh Heupel completed 17 of 27 passes for 275 yards. In all, the Sooners piled up 534 yards while Texas had only 154 total yards.

The slaughter was so complete and so embarrassing that UT head coach Mack Brown apologized to the university, the student body, and the Longhorn fans for the team's performance. On the other hand, senior defensive tackle Ryan Fisher celebrated the big

SOONERS

win by planting a giant OU flag at midfield while senior lineman Al Baysinger hitched a victory ride on the Sooner Schooner.

The whole team gathered "in one relaxed, celebrating mass" for a photo with the scoreboard in the background. The same one that Kempenich looked up to and asked the question of the day: "Dang! What's up with that?"

Life is an ongoing search for answers, and thus whether our life is lived richly or is wasted is largely determined by both the quality and the quantity of the answers we find. Life is indeed one question after another. What's for dinner? Can we afford a new car? What kind of team will OU have this season?

But we also continuously seek answers to questions at another, more crucial level. What will I do with my life? Why am I here? Why does God allow suffering and tragedy?

An aspect of wisdom is reconciling ourselves to and being comfortable with the fact that we will never know all of the answers. Equally wise is the realization that the answers to life's more momentous questions lie within us, not beyond us.

One question overrides all others, the one that Jesus asked Peter: "Who do you say I am?" Peter gave the one and only correct answer: "You are the Son of the Living God." How you answer that question is really the only one that matters, since it decides not just how you spend your life but how you spend eternity.

Age is a question of mind over matter. If you don't mind, it doesn't matter.

-- Satchel Paige

**Only one question in life determines
your eternal fate: Who do you say Jesus is?**

HERO WORSHIP

Read 1 Samuel 16:1-13.

*"Do not consider his appearance or his height, for . . . the
Lord does not look at the things man looks at. . . . The
Lord looks at the heart" (v. 7).*

Roland "Waddy" Young wasn't just a hero on the football field;
he was a true hero off the field too.

In 1938, Young was Oklahoma's first consensus All-America.
He was a tight end and defensive end, a leader of a ferocious defense that gave up only twelve points all season for a 10-0 team.
A versatile athlete, Young wrestled for the Sooners and was the
school's heavyweight boxing champ.

Young was still practicing for the Orange Bowl encounter with
Tennessee when the wrestling team went to Stillwater to take on
Oklahoma State. Young and his teammates emerged from the
locker room to a hearty chorus of hoots and boos, many of them
directed specifically at Young. He turned the insults into laughter
and applause, though, by deftly juggling a trio of oranges.

Young played professional football for two seasons after he left
Norman and then entered the army. He became a member of the
elite flying club who piloted the B-17 bombers in Europe during
World War II. Young flew more than 9,000 combat hours and was
decorated for his distinguished and heroic service.

After the war in Europe ended, Young volunteered to fly in the
Pacific against Japan. He was given command of a squadron of

the new B-29 Super Fortresses.

On Jan. 9, 1945, Young was returning from a successful bombing mission over Tokyo when one of his squadron's planes was losing speed and altitude as it was attacked. He turned his plane, Waddy's Wagon, around to help and flew back into harm's way. His last radio transmission was "We are OK."

Young and his crew never returned. This true American hero was inducted into the College Football Hall of Fame in 1986 and the Oklahoma Sports Hall of Fame in 2007.

A hero is commonly thought of as someone who performs brave and dangerous feats that save or protect someone's life – as Roland "Waddy" Young did during World War II. You figure that excludes you.

But ask your son about that when you show him how to bait a hook, or your daughter when you show up for her dance recital. Look into the eyes of those Little Leaguers you help coach.

Ask God about heroism when you're steady in your faith. For God, a hero is a person with the heart of a servant. And if a hero is a servant who acts to save other's lives, then the greatest hero of all is Jesus Christ.

God seeks heroes today, those who will proclaim the name of their hero – Jesus – proudly and boldly, no matter how others may scoff or ridicule. God knows heroes when he sees them -- by what's in their hearts.

Heroes and cowards feel exactly the same fear; heroes just act differently.
-- Boxing trainer Cus D'Amato

God's heroes are those who remain steady
in their faith while serving others.

STRANGE BUT TRUE

Read Philippians 2:1-11.

"And being found in appearance as a man, he humbled himself and became obedient to death – even death on a cross!" (v. 7)

Strange but true: OU once scored a touchdown by swimming in a creek.

J. Brent Clark tells the story of "The Legendary Game at Cottonwood Creek." OU and the Oklahoma A&M Aggies met for the first time in football in 1904; they played in Guthrie, a neutral site, "hard by the banks of the rain-swollen Cottonwood Creek."

The game was played in harsh, sub-freezing weather. "A gale force north wind erupted, enough to cause the formation of ice crystals on tree limbs and creek banks." Early in the game, the Aggies tried to punt into the teeth of that gale-force wind. The ball went straight up and then was swept backwards.

In those formative years of the game, the ball was in play no matter where it landed and could be retrieved by either team. Thus, when the wind seized the football and propelled it along a foot path, the players from both teams took off after it.

The ball rolled along and right on into the icy waters of Cottonwood Creek where it bobbled quite merrily like a fisherman's cork. While spectators hustled to catch up to the action, the players hesitated only a moment before jumping into the "seven feet deep, swirling creek waters in frenzied search of the ball." They even

SOONERS

included a few players who, in their excitement, jumped in before they realized they couldn't swim.

OU's Ed Cook was an excellent swimmer, so he reached the ball first, clutched it to his chest, swam ashore, and touched the ground with the ball. He thereby scored what is surely the strangest touchdown in Oklahoma football history.

He was not alone in scoring. Every man on the OU team had a touchdown that day in the 75-0 win.

Life is just strange, isn't it? How else to explain tofu, the proliferation of tattoos, and the behavior of teenagers? Isn't it strange that today we have more ways to stay in touch with each other yet are losing the intimacy of personal contact?

And how strange is God's plan to save us? Think a minute about what God did. He could have come roaring down, destroying and blasting everyone whose sinfulness offended him, which, of course, is pretty much all of us. Then he could have brushed off his hands, nodded the divine head, and left a scorched planet in his wake. All in a day's work.

Instead, God came up with a totally novel plan: He would save the world by becoming a human being, letting himself be humiliated, tortured, and killed, thus establishing a kingdom of justice and righteousness that will last forever.

It's a strange way to save the world – but it's true.

It may sound strange, but many champions are made champions by setbacks.

-- Olympic champion Bob Richards

**It's strange but true: God allowed himself
to be killed on a cross to save the world.**

IN THE BAD TIMES

Read Philippians 1:3-14.

"What has happened to me has really served to advance the gospel. . . . Because of my chains, most of the brothers in the Lord have been encouraged to speak the word of God more courageously and fearlessly" (vv. 12, 14).

The women's basketball program at OU was once in such bad shape that school administrators voted to drop the sport.

Following the 1989-90 season, officials saw a losing record, a litany of players' gripes about the coaching staff, and an attendance at home games that usually hovered around 60. They then decided to give what was pretty much a dead program a decent burial and voted to end it.

The program stayed dead for eight days. That's how long it took for a surge of public protest to make its point that the decision was a violation of Title IX. But that didn't cure the ills; it just allowed women's basketball to limp along with the same problems.

When the head coach retired after the 1995-96 season, new associate athletic director Marita Hynes set about the task of finding a coach who could end the bad times. To her surprise, she was blown away by a spunky 5'5" 31-year-old high-school coach with no collegiate coaching experience. That was Sherri Coale.

Eight months pregnant and wearing the only dress she had that still fit, Coale handed each of the interview committee members a pamphlet that detailed how she would put an end to the bad times. "By the end of the meeting, we were all ready to put on our shoes and go play for her," Hynes said.

Coale's first season was so miserable (5-22) that at times after games she could be found with her head in her hands sobbing. After an 8-19 record in 1997-98, though, the bad times were gone for good. Through the 2012-13 season, the Sooner women had been to fourteen straight NCAA tournaments, and Coale was the winningest coach in Big 12 women's basketball history.

Loved ones die. You're downsized. Your biopsy looks cancerous. Your spouse could be having an affair. Hard, tragic times are as much a part of life as breath.

This applies to Christians too. Christianity is not the equivalent of a Get-out-of-Jail-Free card, granting us a lifelong exemption from either the least or the worst pain the world has to offer. While Jesus promises us he will be there to lead us through the valleys, he never promises that we will not enter them.

The question thus becomes how you handle the bad times. You can buckle to your knees in despair and cry, "Why me?" Or you can hit your knees in prayer and ask, "What do I do with this?"

Setbacks and tragedies are opportunities to reveal and to develop true character and abiding faith. Your faithfulness -- not your skipping merrily along through life without pain -- is what reveals the depth of your love for God.

If you coach for 25 years and never win a championship, but you influence three people for Christ, that is success.

— Sherri Coale

**Faithfulness to God requires faith
even in -- especially in -- the bad times.**

FAMILY TIES

Read Mark 3:31-35.

*"[Jesus] said, 'Here are my mother and my brothers!
Whoever does God's will is my brother and sister and
mother'" (vv. 34-35).*

College football teams are often described as being like a family. For one glorious season in 1973, the heart of the Oklahoma defense was quite literally a family.

Many historians still consider that '73 team to be the finest in OU history. The team was part of the probation time from 1973 through 1976. *Sports Illustrated* called the Sooners "The Best Team You'll Never See." The heart of that '73 squad was the defense, which has been called "OU's most suffocating defense ever." In turn, the heart of that defense was "the most amazing brother act in college football history": Lucious, Lee Roy, and Dewey, the Selmon brothers.

They played side by side on the '73 defensive line for that 10-0-1 season marred only by a 7-7 tie with USC. Lucious was the senior All-America nose guard. His sophomore brothers -- not twins -- flanked him on the line. They, too, would be All-Americas.

They grew up in grinding poverty in a tiny frame farmhouse without indoor plumbing or hot water. But they also grew up in a home "charged with familial devotion and self-respect." Around town, folks spoke of the family's devotion to church and school. The little TV set in the living room was always dark from Monday

SOONERS

to Friday. "When Mama said study, we studied," Lucious said. Without a tractor, the boys plowed behind the family horse. They worked as the school janitors before and after class.

Lee Roy was the last of the nine Selmon children, and his dad told an acquaintance he didn't know how he was going to manage what with the price of everything. The friend advised him to quit having children; he did. Barry Switzer later said his advice to the friend would have been to keep his mouth shut.

For the Sooners, the Selmon family wasn't nearly big enough.

Some wit said families are like fudge, mostly sweet with a few nuts. You can probably call the names of your sweetest relatives, whom you cherish, and of the nutty ones too, whom you mostly try to avoid at a family reunion.

Like it or not, you have a family, and that's God's doing. God cherishes the family so much that he chose to live in one as a son, a brother, and a cousin.

One of Jesus' more startling actions was to redefine the family. No longer is it a single household of blood relatives or even a clan or a tribe. Jesus' family is the result not of an accident of birth but rather a conscious choice. All those who do God's will are members of Jesus' family.

What a startling and downright wonderful thought! You have family members out there you don't even know who stand ready to love you just because you're part of God's family.

God Bless Mrs. Selmon!
-- OU student section chant after pre-game prayer (1973-75)

For followers of Jesus, family comes not from a shared ancestry but from a shared faith.

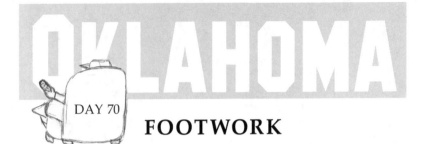

FOOTWORK

Read Isaiah 52:7-12.

"How beautiful on the mountains are the feet of those who bring good news" (v. 7).

Of all things, Sam Bradford began his rehab from major shoulder surgery by concentrating on his feet.

After winning the Heisman Trophy in 2008 as a redshirt sophomore, Bradford opted to come back to Norman for another shot at the national title. In the 2009 season opener against BYU, though, he suffered a shoulder sprain. He missed three games before he returned to the lineup on Oct. 10 and threw for 389 yards in a 33-7 blowout of Baylor. That was as good as it got.

In the Red River Shootout the following week, Bradford was sacked in the first quarter. He landed hard on that injured right shoulder, stood up, and then dropped to his knees. It was his last play as a Sooner; he had a major shoulder separation.

Surgery and a nine-week rehabilitation program in Florida followed. The goal was to rescue Bradford's pro career.

It was the longest he had ever been away from home in his life. He texted family and friends continually, calling on his faith in God to help him through his loneliness and the uncertainty about his shoulder and his future.

His workouts started immediately after his surgery, but at first he never threw a football. Josh Heupel, Bradford's quarterbacks coach at OU, had always stressed to him that poor footwork led to poor throws. So to ease the stress on his shoulder when he did start throwing, Bradford concentrated on his footwork.

After three months, he finally threw a ball. His shoulder held up, and he was the first player taken in the 2010 draft. As a bonus, his excellent footwork helped make him a better quarterback.

Day to day, we rarely pay much attention to our feet. Throw athlete's foot, corns, calluses, bunions, or ingrown toenails into the mix, however, and those aching digits make us a whole lot more aware of them and how important they are.

Even if we are flattered when someone tells us how lovely certain of our body parts are, we probably regard as slightly strange someone's commenting on how pretty and delectable our feet are. Especially if we're men and don't have the advantage of painted toenails.

But Jehovah himself waxes poetic about our pretty feet under one circumstance: when we are hotfooting about delivering the good news of salvation through Jesus Christ. We are commissioned by our Lord not to prop our feet up, but rather to put those feet – flat or otherwise – onto the ground and share with others God's life-changing message of redemption through Christ.

The feet of the gospel's messenger are beautiful because they bear the bearer of the most beautiful message of all: Jesus saves.

If I'd just tried to throw without working on my feet, I probably could have put some more pressure on my shoulder.
-- Sam Bradford, explaining the emphasis on his footwork

Our feet are beautiful when they take us
to people who need the beautiful message
of salvation in Jesus.

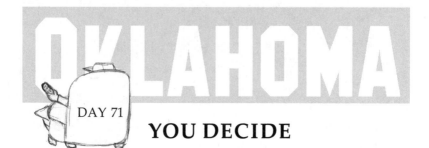

YOU DECIDE

Read John 6:60-69.

"The words I have spoken to you are spirit and they are life. Yet there are some of you who do not believe" (vv. 63b-64a).

Of all the decisions he made as OU's head football coach, Bud Wilkinson said the most important one was to hand-pick Prentice Gautt.

The university had been integrated since 1950, but in 1956, the same wasn't true of the football team. Wilkinson knew it was time. He carefully researched potential players and decided that Gautt, an all-state running back from Oklahoma City, had the temperament and the talent it would take to handle what would come his way. In the fall of 1956, Gautt enrolled as a Sooner football player and broke the color barrier.

All-American guard/linebacker Leon Cross said of the head coach's decision, "Either Coach Wilkinson was a genius in picking Prentice or he was very lucky." Gautt went on to become a two-time All-Big 8 player, an academic All-America, and the MVP of the 1959 Orange Bowl. "In many ways," Gautt said, "I saw myself as just another football player trying to make it at a great program. . . . It was about football and school and teammates."

In 1999, the university's athletic academic center was named after Gautt. On the day of its dedication, he stood on the 50-yard line of Memorial Stadium as a standing ovation cascaded down onto the field. "And it went on and on," recalled athletic director Joe Castiglione. "All of us were standing there, and the tears were running down our cheeks."

Jakie Sandefer, Gautt's roommate on road trips, introduced Gautt at his induction into the Oklahoma Sports Hall of Fame in 2000. He said Prentice Gautt was different, but it had nothing to do with the color of his skin. "He had more class than the rest of us, and he was a better student," he said.

Just exactly what led to Bud Wilkinson's decision in 1956.

The decisions you have made along the way have shaped your life at every pivotal moment. Some decisions you made suddenly and carelessly; some you made carefully and deliberately; some were forced upon you. You may have discovered that some of those spur-of-the-moment decisions have turned out better than your carefully considered ones.

Of all your life's decisions, however, none is more important than one you cannot ignore: What have you done with Jesus? Even in his time, people chose to follow Jesus or to reject him, and nothing has changed; the decision must still be made and nobody can make it for you. Ignoring Jesus won't work either; that is, in fact, a decision, and neither he nor the consequences of your decision will go away.

Carefully considered or spontaneous – how you arrive at a decision for Jesus doesn't matter; all that matters is that you get there.

It was the most significant thing I did when I was coaching.
-- Bud Wilkinson on his deciding for Prentice Gautt

A decision for Jesus may be spontaneous or considered; what counts is that you make it.

GOAL ORIENTED

Read 1 Peter 1:3-12.

"For you are receiving the goal of your faith, the salvation of your souls" (v. 9).

Stacey King had basically washed out at OU, so his less than happy mama decided it was time her son established some goals for his life.

King is a Sooner basketball legend. He starred for OU from 1985-89. A left-handed center, he averaged 17.6 points his junior season in leading the Sooners to the '88 national championship game. As a senior he was first-team All-America and the Big-Eight Player of the Year. He averaged 26.0 points and 10.1 boards. In 2008, his jersey No. 33 was retired.

King didn't exactly get off to a rousing start in Norman, however. He spent his freshman season sitting on the bench, ineligible because of his grades. "When Jack Frost was nipping at my toes, I was in bed," King explained about failing to make it to class his first semester. His mama warned him, "Boy, you'd better go to class or you'll be sitting down next semester." But her son didn't listen. "And sure enough -- boom!" King said. "I'm sitting on the sidelines in my street clothes, cheering like a cheerleader."

As writer Hank Hersch put it, "The King family of Lawton, Okla., is not fond of excuses." Mama wasn't interested in hearing any from her son, and right about then she was not very happy with him.

SOONERS

So she sat him down with pen and paper and ordered him to draw up two lists: one with his goals in life and the other with his priorities. Then she demanded that he explain both lists to her. As King recalled it, "The goals included graduating on time and developing each year as a person both on and off the court." His priorities included studying hard.

His mother told him, "Anytime you think you might want to get off on the wrong track, you take these out and look at them and say I wrote these for my mother." King made the dean's list next semester and was never academically ineligible again.

What are your goals in life? Have you ever thought them out? Or do you just shuffle along living for your paycheck and whatever fun you can seek out instead of pursuing some greater purpose?

Now try this one: What is the goal of your faith life? You go to church to worship God. You read the Bible and study God's word to learn about God and how God wants you to live. But what is it you hope to achieve? What is all that stuff about? For what purpose do you believe that Jesus Christ is God's son?

The answer is actually quite simple: The goal of your faith life is your salvation, and this is the only goal in life that matters. Nothing you will ever seek is as important or as eternal as getting into Heaven and making sure that everybody you know and love will be there too one day.

We didn't have a Leave It to Beaver-type conversation.
  -- Stacey King on when his mother decided to clarify his goals in life

**The most important goal of your life
is to get to Heaven and to help as many people
as you can to get there one day too.**

HANGING IN THERE

Read Mark 14:32-42.

"'Father,' he said, 'everything is possible for you. Take this cup from me. Yet not what I will, but what you will'" (v. 36).

Pryce Macon thought long and hard about it, but he decided to hang in there, not to give up football. What OU got in return was one of the biggest plays of the 2010 season and one of the greatest performances in the history of the Big 12 Championship.

The 2009 season was to be the junior defensive end's long-awaited chance to shine, but he suffered a knee injury and never even got on the field. "It was hard," Macon said. "I was like, 'Dang, maybe I'm not going to get my chance to get out there.'"

Making it harder for Macon was that his roommates -- Adrian Taylor, Gerald McCoy, and Jeremy Beal -- all developed into stars on the defensive line. Macon was ready to quit. Before he did, though, he prayed. He talked it over with his parents and his roommates. Ultimately, he realized one key factor about life: "You start quitting now, it'll be easier to quit later on in life, too."

So he hung in there and went into his senior season (2010) with a new attitude. After spring practice, defensive coordinator Brent Venables said Macon had made as much improvement in as short a time as any player he had ever coached.

It showed in the season. In Oklahoma's first road game, the Sooners were in trouble against Cincinnati. They led by two with the Bearcats in field goal range. Macon sacked the quarterback and forced a fumble that Beal recovered. OU won 31-29.

By the Big 12 Championship game, he was an integral part of the team. He had "one of the best single-game defensive performances of the Bob Stoops era." In the 23-20 win over Nebraska, Macon had five tackles for loss (only one off the school record) and three sacks and forced two fumbles.

"God had a plan for me," Macon said, "and I'm glad I stayed, stuck it out and kept fighting." So were Sooner fans.

Life is tough; it inevitably beats us up and kicks us around some. But life has four quarters, and so here we are, still standing, still in the game. Like Pryce Macon realized, we know that we can never win if we don't finish. We emerge as winners and champions only if we never give up, if we just see it through.

Interestingly, Jesus has been in the same situation. On that awful night in the garden, Jesus understood the nature of the suffering he was about to undergo, and he begged God to take it from him. In the end, though, he yielded to God's will and surrendered his own.

Even in the matter of persistence, Jesus is our example. As he did, we push doggedly and determinedly ahead – following God's will for our lives -- no matter how hard it gets. And we can do it because God is with us.

Pryce [Macon] is a good example of perseverance.
– OU defensive ends coach Bobby Jack Wright

**It's tough to keep going no matter what,
but you have the power of almighty God
to pull you through.**

| DAY 74 | ## CHEAP TRICKS |

Read Acts 19:11-20.

"The evil spirit answered them, 'Jesus I know, and I know about Paul, but who are you?'" (v. 15)

Sooner offensive tackle Byron Bigby once slept through practice but managed to trick the coaches and get away with it.

Nicknamed the "Big Kid" by his teammates. Bigby started as a junior and a senior in 1967 and '68, opening holes for Heisman-Trophy winner Steve Owens. One day, though, Bigby became "the only player in the history of OU to miss a practice completely with no medical or personal reason: he slept through practice!"

The Big Kid's extended dance with the Sandman occurred one rainy spring afternoon when he was a freshman. On the practice field at the time were about eighty freshman and some forty or fifty upperclassmen. Lineman Eddie Lancaster said of the scene, "It was chaotic."

As the wet and muddy players trudged off the field from yet another two-hour practice, somebody noticed that Bigby wasn't there. One player said he probably slept through practice, and the other Sooners laughed. Nobody could do that.

But when they passed the dorm and screamed at Bigby's window and he appeared with an astonished look on his face, they knew. They also knew he was not long for the team.

But the Big Kid had a trick up his big sleeve.

As the players entered the dressing room, Bigby rushed in,

put on his practice gear, and ran outside. He hurried onto the practice field, found a mud puddle, and rolled around in it. Then he scampered back to the dressing room and sat down on a bench. "He had mud all over him and had wet his hair as mock sweat, and he sat there, trying to appear very tired."

The coaches walked in and one of them patted Bigby on the shoulder and said, "Good practice, son!" As Lancaster put it, with that one trick, Bigby became a Sooner practice-field legend.

Scam artists are everywhere — and they love to try to trick us. An e-mail encourages you to send money to some foreign country to get rich. That guy at your front door offers to resurface your driveway at a ridiculously low price. A TV ad promises a pill to help you lose weight without diet or exercise.

You've been around; you check things out before deciding. The same approach is necessary with spiritual matters, too, because false religions and bogus Christian denominations abound. The key is what any group does with Jesus. Is he the son of God, the ruler of the universe, and the only way to salvation? If not, then what the group espouses is something other than the true Word of God.

The good news about Jesus does indeed sound too good to be true. But the only catch is that there is no catch. No trick -- just the truth.

We were all amazed, but the look on [Byron Bigby's] face was so incredible that we just died laughing right there.
            -- Eddie Lancaster on Byron Bigby's sleeping through practice

**God's promises through Jesus sound too good to
be true, but the only catch is that there is no catch.**

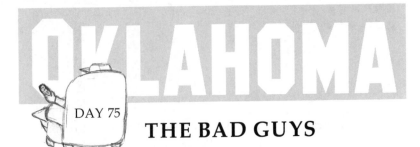

THE BAD GUYS

Read Ephesians 6:10-18.

"Our struggle is not against flesh and blood, but against the rulers, against the authorities, against the powers of this dark world and against the spiritual forces of evil in the heavenly realms" (v. 12).

Rowdy Lundegreen never did see the face of the stranger who tried to kill him.

Lundegreen was well on his way to playing college football at a Texas school until he had a dream one night. He saw himself wrestling and standing in a spotlight surrounded by blackness. He was wearing a singlet that read "Oklahoma." When Lundegreen awoke, he knew Norman was where God wanted him to go and a college wrestler what was God wanted him to be. The dream literally came true at his first dual meet in 1997 when all the lights went out and a spotlight shined on him.

Before his sophomore season, Lundegreen helped a teammate who had recently had knee surgery pick up some things in Plano, Texas. On the way back, though, a truck tire blew out, and they discovered they didn't have a jack. Lundegreen hit the pavement for the two-mile walk back to the last exit and a service station.

As he walked along on the side of the road facing the traffic, a car suddenly swerved right at him with the obvious intention of running him over. Lundegreen dived for the side of the road, bouncing his way down a nearly vertical 40-foot embankment and pretty much destroying an ankle as he went.

He got back on the road and was limping along until a state trooper pulled over. With his torn clothes and his bloody arms and legs, Lundegreen had to tell his story to convince the trooper he was not a criminal. "You don't know how lucky you are," the officer told him. "There's some sort of nut going up and down the highway the last few weeks. A week ago , he ran one guy down."

Just like Rowdy Lundegreen, we never know what evil is all around us. We do know that a just and good God tolerates the existence of evil even if why this is so remains a mystery.

Evil is not intrinsically a part of God's physical world, which God declared to be "good." Rather, evil is a function of the spirit world, of Satan and his minions. Human beings are thus the pawns in an ongoing cosmic struggle between good and evil. The primary battleground is our hearts.

This is why we struggle with evil even after we surrender our lives to Christ. The forces of evil don't concede defeat; they work harder.

The day of God's own choosing will come when all evil will be defeated and goodness will rule unopposed. Not only will the spiritual forces of evil be eradicated, but so will those humans who have aligned themselves with them.

Evil is for losers.

I had to drive two hours back to Norman with the busted ankle.
-- Rowdy Lundegreen on the aftermath of his encounter with evil

Evil may win temporarily – even in your heart –
but to follow Jesus is to live daily
in the knowledge of good's ultimate triumph.

DEBT FREE

Read Colossians 2:8-15.

*"God made you alive with Christ. He forgave us all
our sins, having canceled the written code, with its
regulations, that was against us and that stood opposed
to us; he took it away, nailing it to the cross" (vv. 13-14).*

Daryl Hunt made sure he paid a debt, even if it were only $5.

Hunt, who was 53 when he died in 2010 of a massive heart attack while he was jogging, is a Sooner gridiron legend. A linebacker from 1975-78, he remains OU's all-time leading tackler with 530. He was All-Big Eight three times and was All-America in both 1977 and '78.

One night during his junior season, though, Hunt was in real trouble. An OU law student came out of a Norman night spot to find Hunt stranded in the parking lot with his car out of gas. That was bad enough, but Hunt was obviously under 21, so he was in a situation that might well get him busted by the police.

The law student recognized Hunt as an OU linebacker and asked him if he could help. Hunt told him he had come to pick up a teammate who had called him because he had been drinking too much to drive. When he arrived, however, the football player was gone. He asked to borrow $5 for gas, promising to repay the law student.

The future lawyer handed Hunt the money and gave him a card from his father's business in Oklahoma City. He then pretty much forgot about the whole affair, figuring he had simply done a good deed and made a donation.

About a week later, though, Hunt showed up at the business with fellow linebacker George Cumby. Hunt gave the student's father an envelope that said, "Thanks for the help." When the student arrived at the office, he opened the envelope to find $5 -- and two Texas tickets.

Daryl Hunt remembered his debt -- and paid it with interest.

Debt is a way of life for many. Perhaps you finance your house, your car, your kids' college education, maybe even the furniture you sit on. You put incidental expenses on your credit cards, like that cruise to the Bahamas or your OU season football tickets. Your life is a ledger in which you work to make sure assets exceed liabilities.

In our arrogance and self-centeredness, we often pat ourselves on the back for what we have accomplished, what we have earned despite the amount of debt we have taken on to achieve it. But the biggest debt we all have isn't to a bank or a credit card company; it's to God. We owe him for our lives and everything in it. That includes not just our toys but the people we cherish and the very sunshine that warms us.

How in the world can we possibly repay such a massive debt? By giving that life back to him through faith in Jesus Christ.

The interest that [Daryl] Hunt paid -- repaying a $5 debt with $5 and Texas tickets. That's how we should live our lives.
-- Writer Berry Tramel

**You are deeply in debt to God for everything
you have, but you repay that debt with your faith.**

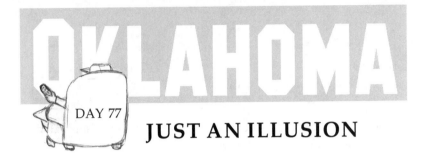

JUST AN ILLUSION

Read Habakkuk 1:2-11.

"Why do you make me look at injustice? Why do you tolerate wrong? Destruction and violence are before me; there is strife, and conflict abounds" (v. 3).

He sat on the Texas bench at the Cotton Bowl. Another time, the head coach spotted him coming into the team hotel at 7 a.m. Ah, but things were not what they seemed.

Guard J.D. Roberts won the Outland Trophy as the nation's top lineman and was All-America as a senior in 1953. In 1993, he was inducted into the College Football Hall of Fame. Roberts was a three-year starter, and the Sooners won the Big Six title all three seasons. The '53 team won its last nine games, thus launching the legendary 47-game win streak.

Following the '52 season, Roberts was back home in Dallas for the holidays. Texas was meeting Tennessee in the Cotton Bowl, and, as Roberts put it, "I wanted to go to the game in the worst way." So he went down to the hotel where the Longhorns were staying, hunted up a coach, and asked him for a pass. "Just come sit on our bench," the coach said. So J.D. Roberts, the All-American Sooner guard, sat on the Texas bench for the 1953 Cotton Bowl.

Head coach Bud Wilkinson had his team stay at a hotel in Oklahoma City the night before home games. The morning of one game during Roberts' junior season, Wilkinson spotted Roberts coming back to the hotel at 7 a.m. He told assistant coach Gomer

Jones to find out exactly what his star guard had been up to.

Jones found Roberts after breakfast and asked him where he had been. "Coach, I've been to church," Roberts replied. "What?" Jones asked. "You want me to believe that? Where's the church?" Roberts told him of a church right down the street and that he always went to mass the morning of the games. After the game, Wilkinson apologized to Roberts for interrogating him so.

So Roberts looked like a Longhorn one time and a party guy the other. In neither case, though, were things what they seemed.

Sometimes in life -- and not just in football -- things aren't what they seem. In our violent and convulsive times, we must confront the possibility of a new reality: that we are helpless in the face of anarchy; that injustice, destruction, and violence are pandemic in and symptomatic of our modern age. Anarchy seems to be winning, and the system of standards, values, and institutions we have cherished appears to be crumbling while we watch.

But we should not be deceived or disheartened. God is in fact the arch-enemy of chaos, the creator of order and goodness and the architect of all of history. God is in control. We often misinterpret history as the record of mankind's accomplishments -- which it isn't -- rather than the unfolding of God's plan -- which it is. That plan has a clearly defined end: God will make everything right. In that day things will be what they seem.

Nothing is ever as good as it seems or as bad as it seems.
-- Former Clemson coach Curley Hallman

The forces of good and decency often seem
helpless before evil's power, but don't be fooled:
God is in control and will set things right.

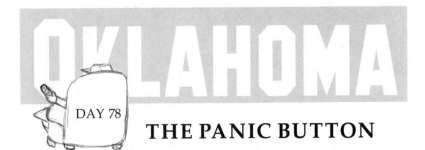

THE PANIC BUTTON

Read Mark 4:35-41.

"He said to his disciples, 'Why are you so afraid? Do you still have no faith?'" (v. 40)

In their biggest game in years, the Sooners fell behind the top-ranked team 14-0 before the first quarter was even over. It sure looked like a good time to panic.

On Oct. 28, 2000, No. 1 met No. 3 in an epic battle that had a lot to say about the eventual national champion. At the time, it was the Nebraska Cornhuskers who were top-ranked, and with their first eleven plays, they looked the part. They rolled up 167 yards and scored two touchdowns on 39- and 37-yard strikes.

"It happened so quickly," said dismayed senior defensive tackle Jeremy Wilson-Guest. "It was like, 'Wow! We've got to buckle up.'"

While the Sooner fans may have felt their throats constricting in fear about this time, the players and coaches said there was no real concern despite the sudden deficit. There was, however, a consensus that Wilson-Guest was right on: They had to buckle up.

They did just that in the second quarter. The Huskers ran fifteen plays and managed a grand total of 16 yards. The Sooners, meanwhile, were having a field day.

Quarterback Josh Heupel was 7 of 10 passing for 149 yards and a touchdown in the period. His 34-yard hookup with sophomore wide receiver Curtis Fagan at the 10:52 mark tied the game at 14.

Less than three minutes later, Josh Norman blocked a punt

SOONERS

that set up Tim Duncan's 19-yard field goal. The onslaught continued when Heupel hit receiver Antwone Savage with a 37-yard completion and Norman followed up with an 8-yard touchdown run. With 2:41 left in the half, OU led 24-14.

Calm and poised throughout, the Sooners went on to win 31-14 to claim the No. 1 spot in the polls for the first time that season.

Have you ever experienced that suffocating sensation of fear escalating into full-blown panic? Maybe that time when you couldn't find your child at the mall or at the beach? Or the heart-stopping moment when you looked out and saw that tornado headed your way?

As the disciples illustrate, the problem with panic is that it debilitates us. Here they were, some professional fishermen in the bunch, and they let a bad storm panic them into helplessness. All they could do was wake up an exhausted Jesus.

We shouldn't be too hard on them, though, because we often make an even more grievous mistake. They panicked and turned to Jesus; we panic and often turn away from Jesus by underestimating both his power and his ability to handle our crises.

We have a choice when fear clutches us: We can assume Jesus no longer cares for us, surrender to it, and descend into panic, or we can remember how much Jesus loves us and resist fear and panic by trusting in him.

No one panicked. We just had to get settled in.
-- Bob Stoops after the Sooners fell behind 14-0

**To plunge into panic is to believe
-- quite wrongly -- that Jesus is incapable
of handling the crises in our lives.**

DAY 79

KEEP OUT!

Read Exodus 26:31-35; 30:1-10.

"The curtain will separate the Holy Place from the Most Holy Place" (v. 26:33).

Even the newspapers called him an outsider, but that didn't keep OU's Walter Emery from crashing the party and winning the NCAA golf championship.

In 1933, Emery was a 20-year-old sophomore at OU who won the 1932 and '33 state intercollegiate golf championship. He also won the individual Big Six Championship and led the Sooners to the team title in Kansas City that season.

Despite his success, though, Emery was literally unknown in the East. He set out with teammate Maurice Hankinson to change all that. The two Sooners hopped in a car and drove a thousand miles to Williamsville, N.Y, for the NCAA Championship.

During qualifying, Emery nearly shot himself out of contention for one of the 32 spots in the championship round. Only a 74 on the second day secured him the 25th spot. Hankinson was 15th.

The qualifiers took each other on with 36 holes of medal play. Hankinson lost early to a Yale golfer. He congratulated the victor, "quickly threw down his bag and traversed the links in search of Emery" to cheer him on. He was a distinct minority. As Emery later said, "I had only three friends in the whole gallery. . . . One was Maurice Hankinson, another was my caddie and the third was some sandy-haired chap I didn't know."

In reporting on the tournament, one paper said Emery "was classed as a decided outsider from the time he qualified." But that "decided outsider" pulled off one upset after another over the better-known golfers from the East.

In the 35th of the 36 holes, Emery blasted from a trap to within one foot of the pin and saved par, thereby defeating his Cornell opponent and becoming the first golfer from west of the Mississippi to win the NCAA title.

That civic club with its membership by invitation only. The bleachers where you sit while others frolic in the sky boxes. That neighborhood you can't afford a house in. You know all about being shut out of some club, some group, some place. "Exclusive" is the word that keeps you out.

The Hebrew people, too, knew about being told to keep out; only the priests could come into the presence of the holy and survive. Then along came Jesus to kick that barrier down and give us direct access to God.

In the process, though, Jesus created another exclusive club; its members are his followers, Christians, those who believe he is the Son of God and the savior of the world. This club, though, extends a membership invitation to everyone in the whole wide world; no one is excluded. Whether you're in or out depends on your response to Jesus, not on arbitrary gatekeepers.

I'd make a good iron second shot, and you'd think there was a funeral around. Nobody said anything.
-- Walter Emery on being the outsider in the '33 NCAA championship

Christianity is an exclusive club, but an invitation is extended to everyone and no one is denied entry.

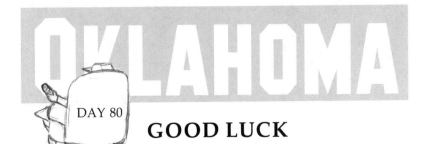

GOOD LUCK

Read Acts 1:15-25.

*"Then they prayed, 'Lord, you know everyone's heart.
Show us which of these two you have chosen.' . . . Then
they cast lots" (vv. 24, 25a).*

Somebody forget to tell the kicker what he was supposed to do
-- and the Sooners went on to win the game as a result.

Last-gasp wins occurred so frequently during the Barry Switzer years at Oklahoma (1973-88) that the phenomenon even had
a name: "Sooner Magic." "Switzer and his Sooners were at their
best when their backs were against the wall." Sometimes, though,
a little luck played a part in that magic as was clearly the case in
the Oklahoma State game of 1983.

The Cowboys led 20-3 with ten minutes to play when quarterback Danny Bradley dropped a little dump pass to Derrick Shepard. He eluded two defenders and went 73 yards for a score. One
possession later, Spencer Tillman's 5-yard touchdown catch and
Earl Johnson's conversion reception made it 20-18 with 2:40 left.

Now Switzer had a big decision to make. At first, he ordered an
onside kick, but then he changed his mind and ordered the kickoff team to cover deep. In all the confusion and excitement, however, nobody got the word of the change in plans to kicker Tim Lashar, a walk-on who had had the job only four weeks.

So he quite dutifully squibbed the onside kick that no other
Sooner player was expecting. The ball caromed off the helmet of

an equally surprised State player and fell right into the hands of defensive back Scott Case at the Cowboy 49.

Given a sudden unexpected jolt, the Sooners moved into Lashar's range. With 1:14 left, he booted a 46-yarder, and the Sooners had a 21-20 win clearly aided by a lucky bounce of the ball. Lashar would go on to set records as an Oklahoma kicker, but this was the longest field goal of his Sooner career.

Ever think sometimes that other people have all the luck? Some guy wins a lottery while you can't get a raise of a few lousy bucks at work. Unlike the State game of '83, the football takes a lucky bounce the other team's way and Oklahoma loses a game. If you have any luck to speak of, it's bad.

To ascribe anything that happens in life to blind luck, however, is to believe that random chance controls everything, including you. But here's the truth: There is no such thing as luck, good or bad. Even when the apostles in effect flipped a coin to pick the new guy, they acknowledged that the lots merely revealed to them a decision God had already made.

It's true that we can't explain why some people skate merrily through life while others suffer in horrifying ways. We don't know why good things happen to bad people and vice versa. But none of it results from luck, unless you want to attribute that name to the force that does indeed control the universe; you know -- the one more commonly called God.

Luck is what happens when preparation meets opportunity.
-- Darrell Royal

**A force does exist that is in charge,
but it isn't luck; it's God.**

A SECOND CHANCE

Read John 7:53-8:11.

"'Then neither do I condemn you,' Jesus declared. 'Go now and leave your life of sin'" (v. 8:11).

Receivers often get second chances, making catches in a game after dropping a ball earlier. Mark Bradley's second chance once came on the same play in which he missed a ball.

On Oct. 31, 2004, the second-ranked Sooners outlasted the 6-1 OSU Cowboys 38-35 in what was described as "epic Bedlam." The game for the ages wasn't decided until Oklahoma State missed a 49-yard field goal with 11 seconds to play.

The game was a shootout, filled with big plays. Freshman running back Adrian Peterson exploded for 249 yards and an 80-yard touchdown run and was named both the Big 12 and the national player of the week. Quarterback Jason White threw three touchdown passes.

Nobody had a bigger day than Bradley did, however. He snared two touchdown passes and ripped off a 50-yard punt return for a score. His second TD reception made for one of the game's more unusual plays in that it took him two tries to catch the ball.

When Bradley arrived in Norman in the summer of 2002, the coaches didn't know what to do with him. He walked on, transferring from Division 1-AA's Arkansas-Pine Bluff. He was an obvious talent with size and speed who equally obviously was in need of some big-game experience.

The coaches first tried him at cornerback before moving him to wide receiver during preseason practice in 2003. In 2004, he was a starter. "He can compete with anybody in the country in terms of his athletic ability," said receivers coach Darrell Wyatt.

Bradley flashed that athletic ability with an acrobatic catch in the second quarter. OSU led 14-7 when White hit him on a crossing pattern. Bradley missed it. The ball caromed off his helmet, high into the air. Then he got a second chance. Without breaking stride, Bradley reached up and gathered the ball in. He turned upfield, and sped 78 yards for a game-tying touchdown.

"If I just had a second chance, I know I could make it work out." Ever said that? If only you could go back and tell your dad one last time you love him, take that job you passed up rather than relocate, or replace those angry shouts at your son with gentle encouragement. If only you had a second chance, a mulligan.

As the story of Jesus' encounter with the adulterous woman illustrates, with God you always get a second chance. No matter how many mistakes you make, God will never give up on you. Nothing you can do puts you beyond God's saving power.

You always have a second chance because with God your future is not determined by your past or who you used to be. It is determined by your relationship with God through Jesus Christ.

God is ready and willing to give you a second chance – or a third chance or a fourth chance – if you will give him a chance.

It was just perfect.
* -- Mark Bradley, laughing about his imperfect, second-chance catch*

**You get a second chance with God
if you give him a chance.**

FEAR FACTOR

Read Matthew 14:22-33.

"[The disciples] cried out in fear. But Jesus immediately said to them: 'Take courage! It is I. Don't be afraid'" (vv. 26-27).

It took a while for Tinker Owens to get over being afraid. At his size, it was understandable.

Charles Wayne Owens, better known as a two-time All-American receiver named Tinker, was quite literally Heisman-Trophy winner Steve Owens' "little" brother. He played football as a sophomore in high school weighing all of 125 pounds and made it up to 155 pounds as a senior safety, wingback, and punter.

The younger Owens arrived at Norman in the fall of 1972. At the time, the freshmen backs, receivers, and quarterbacks ran patterns against the varsity during practice. Owens recalled that when the freshmen would walk from their practice into the stadium, "the varsity players would chant 'fresh meat, fresh meat' just like at a prison." Considering he weighed about 160 pounds and was only 17 years old at the time, Owens' reaction was pretty normal: "I was scared to death."

But the week after the opening win over Utah State, Owens caught three touchdown passes against the varsity in practice. That earned him a promotion for the Oregon game, but he didn't expect to play. Thus, he was completely rattled when head coach Chuck Fairbanks suddenly yelled at him to get in the game, and he had to search frantically for his helmet. He did calm down enough to catch a pass his second play on the field.

Owens' fears still hadn't completely left him by the Texas game. As he walked down the ramp into the Cotton Bowl, Texas guys to his left jawed at him. That was frightful enough, but then "they shot that big cannon and I thought I lost it." The sight of Bevo nearby didn't help either. But as Owens admitted, once the game started, "you forget all of that" and your fears dissipate.

Some fears are universal; others are particular. Speaking to the Rotary Club may require a heavy dose of antiperspirant. Elevator walls may feel as though they're closing in on you. And don't even get started on being in the dark with spiders and snakes during a thunderstorm.

We all live in fear, and God knows this. Dozens of passages in the Bible urge us not to be afraid. God isn't telling us to lose our wariness of oncoming cars or big dogs with nasty dispositions; this is a helpful fear God instilled in us for protection. What God does wish driven from our lives is a spirit of fear that dominates us, that makes our lives miserable and keeps us from doing what we should, such as sharing our faith. In commanding that we not be afraid, God reminds us that when we trust completely in him, we find peace that calms our fears.

I wasn't jawing back because this time I was scared to death of an opponent.
— *Tinker Owens before his first Texas game (1972)*

**You have your own peculiar set of fears,
but they should never paralyze you
because God is greater than anything you fear.**

TOP SECRET

Read Romans 2:1-16.

"This will take place on the day when God will judge men's secrets through Jesus Christ, as my gospel declares" (v. 16).

Bud Wilkinson's Sooners of 1949 were so good that not even a trio of spies could keep them from winning.

Some historians have argued that the '49 squad could still be the best Oklahoma team ever. They were certainly very good. The team went undefeated and finished behind Notre Dame at No. 2 in the final wire polls. They led the nation in rushing defense and were second in rushing offense.

Halfback George "Junior" Thomas took the season-opening kickoff back 95 yards for a touchdown against Boston College (a 46-0 cakewalk), and the Sooners were off and running. They were tested only twice, one of them a 20-14 win over Texas, a game so physical that tackle Wade Walker was knocked out on his feet and kept wandering into the Longhorn huddle.

After the 10-0 season and another Big Six title, the Sooners accepted an invitation to play LSU in the Sugar Bowl. Wilkinson had his team hole up and practice in Biloxi, Miss. After the practice of Dec. 30, the head coach received a call from a local man who informed him his last two workouts had been spied upon.

It seems three men had hidden under a tarpaulin on the roof of a nearby garage. "That was the only time I ever saw Bud real angry," said Sooner assistant Pop Ivy. "His face was white."

The next day Wilkinson led an expedition that included a Biloxi policeman, and they moved in on the spies. Sooner quarterback Darrell Royal identified one of the voyeurs from a photograph as a former LSU tackle. LSU's athletic director denied any connection to the trio.

Whatever information the men gathered didn't help much. The Sooners won easily 35-0.

As Bud Wilkinson was about some of his football plays, we have to be vigilant about the personal information we prefer to keep secret. Much information about us -- from credit reports to what movies we rent -- is readily available to prying and persistent persons. In our information age, people we don't know may know a lot about us — or at least they can find out. And some of them may use this information for harm.

While diligence may allow us to be reasonably successful in keeping some secrets from the world at large, we should never deceive ourselves into believing we are keeping secrets from God. God knows everything about us, including the things we wouldn't want proclaimed at church. All our sins, mistakes, failures, shortcomings, quirks, prejudices, and desires – God knows all our would-be secrets.

But here's something God hasn't kept a secret: No matter what he knows about us, he loves us still.

It didn't fire us up. We were ready to play anyhow.
— Cocaptain Stan West on the spying incident

**We have no secrets before God,
and it's no secret that he nevertheless loves us still.**

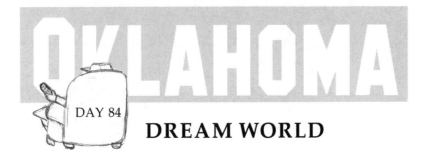

DAY 84

DREAM WORLD

Read Joshua 3.

*"All Israel passed by until the whole nation had completed
the crossing on dry ground" (v. 17b).*

The dream came true for Jennifer Stewart. Well, sort of.

Each year while she was growing up, Stewart and her dad made
the short drive from Yukon to Hall of Fame Stadium in Oklahoma
City for the Women's College World Series. "Jennifer was always
wanting to see the big girls play out there," her dad said.

And she was always dreaming of being one of them out there
on that field playing for that national championship. "You hope
you're out there one of these days, but it's so far out of sight," she
said. "It's a dream."

On Monday, May 27, 2000, Stewart realized that dream. She
pitched the Sooners to a 3-1 win over UCLA and the national title.
The sophomore had already pitched OU's three other games in
the tournament, so she didn't really think she'd be starting the
title game. During batting practice, though, head coach Patty
Gasso came up to her and asked her if she could go. "I'm ready,"
Stewart said. "I'll get the job done. Give me the ball."

Gasso did and Stewart did. She scattered eight hits, faced only
28 batters, and allowed only two runners to get to third base in
the win. She was named the MVP of the World Series.

"Who could've written it this way?" she said about her dreams
coming true. She certainly didn't.

That's because when Stewart dreamed as a little girl of playing in the college world series, she never saw herself wearing crimson and cream. Instead, her softball dreams came in shades of blue and yellow and red, the colors of the West Coast schools that dominated women's softball.

The dream that came true for Stewart, though, was better than the ones that didn't, those in which she wore a uniform other than Oklahoma's. "I can't believe it," she said after the title game.

No matter how tightly or how doggedly we cling to our dreams, devotion to them won't make them a reality. Moreover, the cold truth is that all too often dreams don't come true even when we put forth a mighty effort. The realization of dreams generally results from a head-on collision of persistence and timing.

But what if our dreams don't come true because they're not the same dreams God has for us? That is, they're not good enough and, in many cases, they're not big enough.

God calls us to great achievements because God's dreams for us are greater than our dreams for ourselves. Could the Israelites, wallowing in the misery of slavery, even dream of a land of their own? Could they imagine actually going to such a place?

The fulfillment of such great dreams occurs only when our dreams and God's will for our lives are the same. Our dreams should be worthy of our best – and worthy of God's involvement in making them come true.

Every kid dreams of being a part of this game.
-- Jennifer Stewart on pitching in the national title game

If our dreams are to come true, they must be worthy of God's involvement in them.

DAY 85

BIG DEAL

Read Ephesians 3:1-13.

*"His intent was that now, through the church, the
manifold wisdom of God should be made known" (v. 10).*

For Bob Stoops and his coaches, it was no big deal. It sure was
to everybody else -- especially to Alabama.

"It" was a decision the Oklahoma head coach made in the game
of Sept. 6, 2003, against the Crimson Tide. The top-ranked Sooners
led only 13-10 in the third quarter, and the Bama defense had shut
them down, forcing a punt on 4th-and-10 from the OU 31. That's
when the Sooner coaches decided it was time to pull off a big play.

"I just felt at that time -- boom!" said Chuck Long, the offensive
coordinator. "We needed to go for the jugular and get this game
back in our hands." So -- with a surprising degree of confidence
-- the coaches decided to go with a fake punt. "They had no prayer
of stopping it if we got the look we wanted," said Mike Stoops,
the team's codefensive coordinator.

The head Sooner, who made the final decision, shrugged off
the notion of taking a gamble. "You've got to do what you feel you
need to do," he said. "I don't know how else to explain it."

All those disclaimers notwithstanding, what resulted was a
play so big that it went a long way toward determining the out-
come of this clash between the two traditional powerhouses.

Punter Blake Ferguson sure felt it was a big deal. "I saw them
come out with the fake punt (call), and I could not believe it," he

said. As Mike Stoops had hoped, the Sooners got the look they wanted, and Alabama indeed couldn't stop it. Ferguson lobbed a short pass to reserve defensive back Michael Thompson, who was wide open out in the right flat.

Thompson added some excitement to the play by bobbling the ball before he secured it. He turned upfield and went 22 yards for a first down. The play proved to be really big when Jason White followed up by hitting Brandon Jones with a 47-yard touchdown pass that clinched the 20-13 Oklahoma win.

"Big deals" are important components of the unfolding of our lives. Our wedding, childbirth, a new job, a new house, key OU games, even a new car. In many ways, what we regard as a big deal is what shapes not only our lives but our character.

One of the most unfathomable anomalies of faith in America today is that while many people profess to be die-hard Christians, they disdain involvement with a local church. As Paul tells us, however, the Church is a very big deal to God; it is at the heart of his redemptive work; it is a vital part of his eternal purposes.

The Church is no accident of history. It isn't true that Jesus died and all he wound up with for his troubles was the stinking Church. It is no consolation prize.

Rather, the church is the primary instrument through which God's plan of cosmic and eternal salvation is worked out. And it doesn't get any bigger than that.

To head coach Bob Stoops, it's just another play.
        -- Assistant coach Kevin Wilson on the fake punt call

**To disdain church involvement is to assert
that God doesn't know what he's doing.**

THE PIONEER SPIRIT

Read Luke 5:1-11.

*"So they pulled their boats up on shore, left everything
and followed him" (v. 11).*

He sure didn't look like a trailblazing pioneer of college athletics, but he was, this bespectacled English professor.

V.L. Parrington stepped off a train in Norman in September 1897 to take up his post as an instructor of English literature at the University of Oklahoma. The event marked "the true arrival of college football to the Oklahoma Territory and its university."

Student Jack Harts had organized a team in 1895 that played a single game. (See Devotion No. 1.) Students then formed a team in 1896, but "it was an informal undertaking at best" with no coach and two games against Norman High School.

Parrington had played football while he was a student at Harvard and took away from his experience the conviction that "football contributed to the well-rounding of the college man." Thus, he eagerly accepted the assignment of football coach from David Ross Boyd, the university president.

While the players were "raw-boned, boot-shod, shy young fellows," the new football coach was anything but. Parrington was "a well-groomed, genteel, eccentric bachelor" who wore elegant, well-pressed tweeds and rolled his own cigarettes, "much to the consternation of Norman's church folk."

Parrington's debut "as the university's first legitimate football coach" took place on Thanksgiving 1897 against the same bunch from Oklahoma City that had beaten OU's first team in 1895. His team employed the cross-blocking technique Parrington had seen at Harvard and dominated the line of scrimmage. The university won easily 16-0.

This pioneer coached for four seasons, compiling a 9-2-1 record. He gave up coaching after that because it interfered with a heavy teaching load, though he remained as athletic director.

Going to a place in your life you've never been before requires a willingness to take risks and face uncertainty head-on. You may have never helped start a football program at a university, but you've had your moments when your latent pioneer spirit manifested itself. That time you changed careers, ran a marathon, volunteered at a homeless shelter, or went back to school.

While attempting new things invariably begets apprehension, the truth is that when life becomes too comfortable and too familiar, it gets boring. The same is true of God, who is downright dangerous because he calls us to be anything but comfortable as we serve him. He summons us to continuously blaze new trails in our faith life, to follow him no matter what. Stepping out on faith is risky all right, but the reward is a life of accomplishment, adventure, and joy that cannot be equaled anywhere else.

The scholarly Parrington laid a significant portion of the foundation for the giant strides in Oklahoma football which were to come.
-- Writer J. Brent Clark

Unsafe and downright dangerous, God calls us
out of the place where we are comfortable to a life
of adventure and trailblazing in his name.

DAY 87

GOOD-BYE

Read John 13:33-38.

"My children, I will be with you only a little longer" (v. 33a).

Barry Switzer didn't get to say good-bye to his friend and mentor, but he wasn't alone. The man was OU's head football coach.

The university's hiring of Jim Mackenzie in 1966 almost didn't happen. For one thing, the school president failed for a week to reach Mackenzie by phone to arrange an interview. Only then did the university's top man discover he was calling another Jim Mackenzie, a student who was on semester break. Once the interview was arranged, Mackenzie flew on a puddle-jumper from Dallas but slept right through his stop in Oklahoma City and had to scramble to call OU officials to apologize.

But he was hired, and his first team went 6-4 in 1966, which "was a positive indicator" after a rough '65 season. His recruiting class included three first-round NFL draft picks (Steve Owens, Jim Files, and Steve Zabel). Optimism was high.

On April 27, 1967, as he headed on a recruiting trip, Mackenzie stuck his head in Switzer's office. The young assistant was on his defensive staff. "I'm going to get us a quarterback," the head man said. "Promise me one thing. Don't run anybody off today." Switzer said he wouldn't and then wished Mackenzie good luck. "He walked out and I never saw him again," Switzer said.

Mackenzie was apparently feeling all right that evening when his return flight landed. At home around midnight, though, his recurring chest pains returned, and he was suddenly stricken by a massive heart attack. OU trainer Ken Rawlinson called Switzer about 1 a.m. with the news, and he rushed to the hospital. It was too late. Jim Mackenzie was dead; he was 37.

More than six hundred people, including Switzer and his fellow coaches, attended funeral services for their fallen friend, saying what good-byes they could.

You've stood by a grave to offer a heartwrenching good-bye. Or grabbed a last-minute hug before a plane leaves. Maybe it was a child leaving home for the first time or your best friends moving halfway across the country. It's an extended separation or the permanent one of death, and good-byes hurt.

Jesus felt the pain of parting too. Throughout his brief ministry, Jesus had been surrounded by and had depended upon his friends and confidants, the disciples. About to leave them, he gathered them for a going-away supper and gave them a heads-up about what was about to happen. In the process, he offered them words of comfort. What a wonderful friend he was! Even though he was the one who was about to suffer unimaginable agony, Jesus' concern was for the pain his friends would feel.

But Jesus wasn't just saying good-bye. He was on his mission of providing the way through which none of us would ever have to say good-bye again.

I'll never forget, that was the last statement Jim Mackenzie made to me.
— Barry Switzer on his final, brief conversation with his friend

**Through Jesus, we will see the day
when we say good-bye to good-byes.**

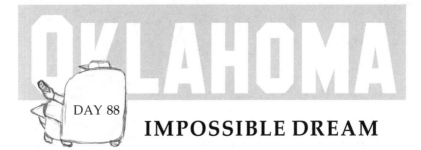

IMPOSSIBLE DREAM

Read Matthew 19:16-26.

"Jesus looked at them and said, 'With man this is impossible, but with God all things are possible'" (v. 26).

Impossible. Nobody wins four straight basketball games by one point. The Sooners of 2005-06 did it, though.

That streak from Feb. 18, 2006, through Feb. 27 became possible only because the Sooners pulled it off, but much about it still seems impossible even in retrospect. For instance, OU beat Iowa State 83-82 when junior guard Michael Neal scored a career-high 29 points. But here's the impossible part. State led by seven points with 58 seconds to play, and Neal scored nine points in those 58 seconds. The last three came on a trio of free throws with 8.4 remaining after he kept the ball in play with an offensive rebound.

The second game in the impossible streak was a 71-70 win over Texas Tech on Feb. 20. The winning field goal this time came with 4.5 seconds left to play on a left-handed tip-in from senior forward Kevin Bookout. Since Bookout played at 6-8, the tip-in wasn't particular remarkable. What made it so, however, was that he did it left handed. At the time, he was wearing a cast on his left hand because of a fracture suffered -- in the last Texas Tech game.

The third game in the impossible streak was a one-point win over Kansas State on Feb. 25. What made this victory improbable if not impossible was that it was by the exact 71-70 score of the Texas Tech game.

SOONERS

The impossible streak went to four on Feb. 27 with an improbable 67-66 win over Oklahoma State. The lead changed hands three times in the final 22 seconds, but State apparently had the game won at 66-65. As the final second ticked away, Terrell Everett was forced to heave a 30-foot prayer. Impossibly, though, he was fouled right before the buzzer sounded. So with 0:00.6 on the clock, the senior guard hit a pair of charity shots for the win.

Four straight wins by one point. Impossible. Consider this, too: The Sooners won seven games that season by one point.

Let's face it. Any pragmatic person, no matter how deep his faith, has to admit that we have succeeded in turning God's beautiful world into an impossible mess. The only hope for this dying, sin-infested place lies in our Lord's return to set everything right.

But we can't just give up and sit around praying for Jesus' return, as glorious a day as that will be. Our mission in this world is to change it for Jesus. We serve a Lord who calls us to step out in faith into seemingly impossible situations. We serve a Lord so audacious that he inspires us to believe that we are the instruments through which God does the impossible.

Changing the world may indeed seem impossible. Changing our corner of it, however, is not. It is, rather, a very possible, doable act of faith.

The difference between the impossible and the possible lies in a person's determination.
-- Former major league manager Tommy Lasorda

With God, nothing is impossible,
including changing the world for Jesus.

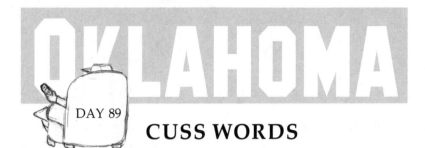

CUSS WORDS

Read Psalm 10.

"[The wicked man's] mouth is full of curses and lies and threats; trouble and evil are under his tongue" (v. 7).

Port Robertson didn't curse. After all, he had promised the Lord.

Robertson is a true OU legend. Across four decades at the university, he was a teacher, a coach, and a leader. He coached the OU wrestling team for 15 years and turned out three national champions. He was also an assistant football coach for 19 years. It was as the athletic guidance counselor from 1954 to 1986, though, that Robertson made his most memorable mark.

Robertson was the disciplinarian, who once said of his players that if they needed discipline, he would loan them some. He was the "away-from-home father of hundreds of Sooners, teaching them to study, to go to class, and subsequently, graduate." As Eddie Lancaster, a lineman in the 1960s, put it, "Port was an angel given to a bunch of boys to drive us to manhood -- and we all loved him as our own father."

For an OU football player, the scariest sight of all was a yellow piece of paper taped to his dormitory door that summoned him to PGR's office. Some transgression was involved that inevitably required running the stadium steps -- 72 rows up and 72 rows down -- over and over again. Until the truant threw up whatever meal had preceded the punishment.

Robertson was a bona fide hero. He was credited with saving

many lives in the Normandy invasion. A few weeks later, he was wounded and struggled with hearing loss the rest of his life. He was also scarred on the left side of his face, which most folks assumed was the result of his collegiate wrestling career.

Despite receiving the Silver Star for gallantry and heroism, Robertson rarely spoke of the war. Once he did, though. Wade Walker, an All-American lineman in the 1940s who later became OU's athletic director, asked Robertson one time why he never, ever cursed. "Well, I made a deal with the Lord at Normandy," Robertson replied. "And I have tried to live up to that promise."

We live in a coarsened culture where words no one would utter in polite society a few decades ago now spew from our music and our television sets—and our own mouths. Honestly answer these indelicate questions: With what name did you christen that slow driver you couldn't pass? What unflattering words did you have for that stubborn golf ball that wouldn't stay in the fairway? And what four-letter words do you sprinkle liberally in your conversations with people whom you want to think of you as "cool"?

Some argue that profane language is really harmless expression. It is in reality quite damaging, though, because of what its use reveals about the speaker: a lack of character, a lack of vocabulary, and a lack of respect for others and reverence for God.

The words you speak reveal what's in your heart, and what God seeks there is love and gentleness, not vileness.

I never recall him swearing or doing anything out of character.
-- OU wrestler and lineman Dick Gwinn on Port Robertson

Our words -- including profane ones --
expose what's in our hearts.

LESSON LEARNED

Read Psalm 143.

"Teach me to do your will, for you are my God" (v. 10).

Football was just one tool Joe Baker used to teach his rambunctious younger brother some discipline.

Lewis Baker grew up in a broken home in a neighborhood rampant with drugs and violence. He spent the summer before his sixth-grade year with Joe, his wife, and three daughters in Dallas. The visit eventually became permanent.

The older brother gave his younger sibling two years to acclimate himself to the household. Then the rules changed. "Everything starts in high school," Joe said. "The choices you make beginning then, you have to live with for a long time." So that's when the lessons in discipline kicked in.

For instance, Lewis recalled the night that his brother stormed into his room and roused him out of bed. Lewis had left crumbs on the kitchen table, and Joe wanted the table cleaned right then. Joe "was super hard on me," Lewis said. "If I went to school and didn't make my bed, he'd go nuts when I got home."

Joe believed that organized athletics taught discipline. So when Lewis entered the ninth grade, Joe encouraged him to try out for football at his new school, which was fielding a team for the first time. He was one of the few freshmen not to make the varsity.

Before Lewis' junior year, though, the coaches moved him to linebacker, and he excelled. Joe and he were fighting at home, however, as Joe continued to insist on discipline. Lewis moved in with his mother for a while, then moved in with a football team-mate instead of living with Joe.

After several months away, though, Lewis began to realize why his older brother was so hard on him. "I didn't see it then. I see it now," he said.

Lewis Baker learned his brother's lesson so well that in 2007 he was a senior at OU, a starting outside linebacker, and a team captain. He earned All-Big 12 Honorable Mention honors.

Learning about anything in life requires both education and experience. Education is the accumulation of facts that we call knowledge; experience is the acquisition of wisdom and discernment, which add purpose and understanding to our knowledge.

The most difficult way to learn is trial and error: dive in blindly and mess up. The best way to learn is through example coupled with a set of instructions: Someone has gone ahead of you and has written down all the information you need to follow.

In teaching us the way to live godly lives, God chose the latter method. He set down in his book the habits, actions, and attitudes that make for a way of life in accordance with his wishes. He also sent us Jesus to explain and to illustrate.

God teaches us not only how to exist but how to live. We just need to be attentive students.

Now I see Joe was just trying to teach me discipline. I really appreciate him for that.
        — Lewis Baker in 2007 as a senior linebacker and team captain

To learn from Jesus is to learn what life is all about and how God means for us to live it.

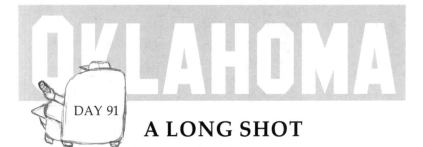

A LONG SHOT

Read Matthew 9:9-13.

"[Jesus] saw a man named Matthew sitting at the tax collector's booth. 'Follow me,' he told him, and Matthew got up and followed him" (v. 9).

When they started the season 0-6, the OU baseball team of 1951 was a long shot to even have a winning season. Yet, they wound up national champions and made College World Series history.

The Sooners did rally somewhat from that 0-6 start, but with the season three-quarters over they still were only 6-9. What didn't show up in that lousy record, though, was that the team was hot. They finished the regular season with a 12-9 record and were the champions of the Big Seven with a 10-1 league record.

That momentum carried them right on to Omaha and the College World Series. Still, the baseball powerhouses gathered there must have looked at their 15-9 record and snickered a little. The Sooners were pesky long shots at best.

They were pesky to Ohio State in their first game, winning a 9-8 thriller in 10 innings despite committing six errors and leaving 16 men on base. In the second game, Jim Waldrip walked fifteen batters but gave up only two hits to beat Springfield (Mass.) 7-1.

The long shots promptly marched right on into the championship game of the double elimination tournament by beating Southern Cal 4-1. Floyd Murphy scattered eight hits; the Sooner defense helped him out by turning four double plays.

That win pitted OU against Tennessee for the title. OU's Jack Shirley held the Vols to two runs on only three hits while center fielder Charley Pugsley delivered the key hit. With the game tied at 2 and two out in the top of the eighth inning, he singled to center to score third baseman Ray Morgosh with the game-winning run.

The long shots from Norman became the first team in College World Series history to win the title without a loss in Omaha.

Like the '51 Sooners, Matthew the tax collector was a long shot. In his case, he was an unlikely person to be a confidant of the Son of God. While we may not get all warm and fuzzy about the IRS, our government's revenue agents are nothing like Matthew and his ilk. He bought a franchise, paying the Roman Empire for the privilege of extorting, bullying, and stealing everything he could from his own people. Tax collectors of the time were "despicable, vile, unprincipled scoundrels."

And yet, Jesus said only two words to this lowlife: "Follow me." Jesus knew that this long shot would make an excellent disciple.

It's the same with us. While we may not be quite as vile as Matthew was, none of us can stand before God with our hands clean and our hearts pure. We are all impossibly long shots to enter God's Heaven. That is, until we do what Matthew did: get up and follow Jesus.

They weren't supposed to be there [the College World Series]. They weren't even supposed to be that good.
*   -- SoonerSports.com on the '51 Sooners*

Only through Jesus does our status change
from being long shots to enter God's Kingdom
to being heavy favorites.

PAY YOUR RESPECTS

Read Mark 8:31-38.

"He then began to teach them that the Son of Man must suffer many things and be rejected by the elders, chief priests and teachers of the law, and that he must be killed" (v. 31).

Despite being perhaps the most famous athlete his hometown has ever produced, Tom Wort gets no respect there. They've never even heard of him.

After a redshirt season in 2009, Wort became the starting middle linebacker for the Big-12 champions as a freshman. Several publications named him second-team Freshman All-America. In 2011, he was honorable mention All-Big 12. He had two interceptions, including one in the 31-14 defeat of Iowa in the Insight Bowl.

Wort's hometown in OU media information is listed as New Braunfels, Texas, but there's more to the story than that. His family arrived in Texas via Rhode Island, but that's not the whole story either. Until Wort was 14, his hometown was Crawley, England, a market town located some 30 miles south of London.

Wort has kept his strong allegiance to his hometown and has always desired to make his town and his home country proud of him. "It's a dream of mine to be recognized back there," he said.

It hasn't worked out that way, though.

It's not that Crawley has produced one sports star after another. Until Wort, perhaps its most famous sporting son was boxer Alan

Minter, who won a bronze medal at the 1972 Olympics. Nevertheless, Crawley hasn't paid much -- really any -- attention to Wort's achievements. An informal survey in 2011 at the local mall uncovered the shocking truth: Nobody had even heard of Wort.

The problem lies in the game Wort plays. Despite some inroads, only relatively few British sports fans regard American college football as a serious pursuit. "I know it's going to be tough, but bringing football home to England would be amazing," Wort said.

First of all, though, he'd settle for a little respect back home.

Rodney Dangerfield made a good living as a comedian with a repertoire that was basically only countless variations on one punch line: "I don't get no respect." Dangerfield was successful because he struck a chord with his audience. No one wants to play football for a program that no one respects. You want the respect, the esteem, and the regard that you feel you've earned.

But more often than not, you don't get it. Still, you shouldn't feel too badly; you're in good company. In the ultimate example of disrespect, Jesus – the very Son of God -- was treated as the worst type of criminal. He was arrested, bound, scorned, ridiculed, spit upon, tortured, condemned, and executed.

God allowed his son to undergo such treatment because of his high regard and his love for you. You are respected by almighty God! Could anyone else's respect really matter?

It's frustrating to be unknown in England for what I'm doing at OU.
-- Tom Wort

You may not get the respect you deserve,
but at least nobody's spitting on you
and driving nails into you as they did to Jesus.

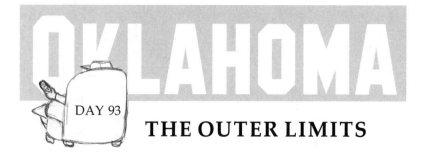

THE OUTER LIMITS

Read Genesis 18:1-15.

"Is anything too hard for the Lord?" (v. 14a)

October 14, 2000 in Manhattan, Kansas. That's the day when and the place where the Sooners kicked the lid off the limits that had held their program down and opened it up to all sorts of possibilities -- including a national championship.

Rarely is a football program able to point to the exact game that either established or re-established its position among college football's elite. The Sooners had just such a moment when they took on second-ranked Kansas State on Oct. 14, 2000.

Headed into that game, the Wildcats, not the Sooners were the big bad boys, the owners of a 25-game home winning streak and the nation's top-ranked defense to go with that lofty spot in the opinion polls. Not since 1992 had the Sooners beaten K-State. When the game was over, though, a new bully had announced itself to the world.

K-State's plan was obvious: use that great defense to shut down OU's rushing attack. They succeeded, holding the Sooner backs to a meager 11 yards. There was a problem, though. "Apparently," said OU offensive coordinator Mark Mangino, "they forgot No. 14 was back there." No. 14 was senior quarterback Josh Heupel; he shredded that vaunted defense for 374 yards passing.

K State led early 7-3, but J.T. Thatcher's 93-yard kickoff return vaulted the Sooners into a 10-7 lead and they never trailed again,

SOONERS

jumping out to a 31-14 halftime lead K-State couldn't overcome.

Sophomore receiver Damian Mackey knew exactly what the 41-31 win meant to the program. "Now, I think the country understands," he said. "OU is here." A cluster of Sooner fans also appreciated that as a result of this game they were allowed to dream as they had not been for some time. They rushed onto the field, chanting, "We're No. 1." Turns out, they were right.

You've probably never tried a whole bunch of things you've dreamed about doing at one time or another. Like starting your own business. Going back to school. Campaigning for elected office. Running a marathon.

But what holds you back? Perhaps you hesitate because you see only your limitations, both those you've imposed on yourself and those of which others constantly remind you. But maybe as those Sooners of 2000 did, it's time you ignored what everybody says. Maybe it's time to see yourself the way God does.

God sees you as you are and also as you can be. In God's eyes, your possibilities are limitless. The realization of those latent possibilities, however, depends upon your depending upon God for direction, guidance, and strength. While you may quail in the face of the challenge that lies before you, nothing is too hard for the Lord.

You can free yourself from that which blights your dreams by depending not on yourself but on God.

Welcome back.
> *-- K-State fan to celebrating Sooner fans after the 2000 game*

**Pray like everything depends upon God;
work like everything depends upon you.**

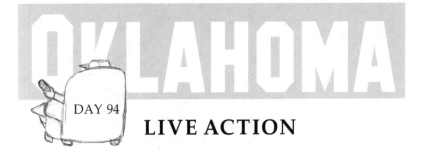

LIVE ACTION

Read James 2:14-26.

"Faith by itself, if it is not accompanied by action, is dead"
(v. 17).

The word had already spread across the country: the King was dead. But then came some inspiring talk that ignited a last-half comeback.

On Nov. 3, 1956, Oklahoma's winning streak of 35 games "was upon its deathbed." Playing in bone-chilling cold in Boulder, the Colorado Buffaloes led the Sooners 19-6 at halftime.

The team gathered in the tiny Quonset hut that served as the visitor's locker room, and a livid head coach Bud Wilkinson went right to work. "Gentlemen," he said, "the jerseys you are wearing are part of the great tradition of Oklahoma.... You do not deserve to wear those jerseys." Then he ordered the players to take them off and left them trembling in the cold semidarkness.

After twenty minutes or so, Wilkinson returned. Calmer by now, he stood "with his nose a few inches from a naked light bulb." He told his team to forget the first half and put their minds to winning the second half, which they could do by three touchdowns. He finished his talk by saying, "Gentlemen, there is only one person who believes you are going to win this game. That person is me." Then he left again.

Senior captains Jerry Tubbs and Ed Gray stood up and finished off the talk with a call to action. "Okay," they said. "Let's go out and get it done."

The players "practically knocked down a steel door as they poured out of the Quonset Hut." Some of them made the trip up the tunnel with their shoulder pads flapping; they were so fired up they had forgotten to put their jerseys back on.

With the pep talk from Wilkinson still ringing in their ears, the Sooners dominated the last half to take a 27-19 win and keep alive what would eventually become the historic 47-game win streak.

Talk is cheap. Consider your neighbor or coworker who talks without saying anything, who makes promises she doesn't keep, who brags about his own exploits, who can always tell you how to do something but never shows up for the work. You know that speech without action just doesn't cut it. Despite one of the sports's greatest halftime pep talks, the Sooners of '56 still had to win the Colorado game with their actions on the field.

That principle applies in the life of a person of faith too. Merely declaring our faith isn't enough, however sincere we may be. It is putting our faith into action that shouts to the world of the depth of our commitment to Christ.

Even Jesus didn't just talk, though he certainly did his share of preaching and teaching. Rather, his ministry was a virtual whirlwind of activity. As he did, so are we to change the world by doing. Anybody can talk about Jesus, but it is when we act for him that we demonstrate how much we love him.

Jesus Christ is alive; so should our faith in him be.

You can motivate players better with kind words than with a whip.
-- Bud Wilkinson

Faith that does not reveal itself in action is dead.

DAY 95

BONE TIRED

Read Matthew 11:27-30.

"Come to me, all you who are weary and burdened, and I will give you rest" (v. 11).

The offensive coordinator wasn't too happy that Steve Owens had insisted on a time out because he was tired.

Owens was a two-time All-America and a three-time All-Big Eight selection who won the Heisman Trophy in 1969. He set an NCAA record that still stands by rushing for at least 100 yards in seventeen straight games. He was inducted into the College Football Hall of Fame and the Oklahoma Sports Hall of Fame in 1991.

The last game of Owens' storied career was on Nov. 29, 1969, against Oklahoma State. The offense was ball control, built around the workhorse back. "We just knew we could wear defenses down in the second half," Owens said. "It was a burden at times."

Never before as on this day, however. The Sooners were behind late in the game and were backed up deep. Owens had carried the ball 25 times in the third quarter alone. "Can you imagine that today?" he later asked.

Nevertheless, the Sooners moved away from their goal line in typical fashion: They gave the ball to Owens. He ran a sweep for his sixth straight carry and was so tired that he told quarterback Jack Mildren to call a time out, which he did.

Mildren trotted to the sideline where he put on the headphones to chat with a most unhappy Barry Switzer, the offensive coordinator. His offense had momentum, and the time out had broken it. Switzer basically told Mildren to tell Owens that "he could rest after the game, but he's not done carrying the ball yet."

Switzer was true to his word and showed no consideration for how tired Owens may have thought he was. Owens ran the ball six straight times after the time out -- that was twelve carries in a row -- and scored. Oklahoma won 28-27, and Owens set a school record that still stands by carrying the ball 55 times in the game.

The everyday struggles and burdens of life beat us down and tire us out. They may be enormous; they may be trivial with a cumulative effect. But they wear us out, so much so that we now have a name for our exhaustion: chronic fatigue syndrome.

Doctors don't help too much. Sleeping pills can zonk us out; muscle relaxers can dull the weariness. Other than that, it's drag on as usual until we can collapse exhaustedly into bed.

Then along comes Jesus, as usual offering hope and relief for what ails us, though in a totally unexpected way. He says take my yoke. Whoa, there! Isn't a yoke a device for work? Exactly. Our mistake is in trying to do it all alone. Yoke ourselves to Jesus, and the power of almighty God is at our disposal to do the heavy lifting for us.

God's strong shoulders and broad back can handle any burdens we can give him. We just have to let them go.

Easy. Coach Switzer makes me carry it 100 times a day during practice.
-- Steve Owens, asked how he could carry the ball 55 times in a game

Tired and weary are a way of life
only when we fail to accept Jesus' invitation
to swap our burdens for his.

A DOG'S LIFE

Read Genesis 6:11-22; 8:1-4.

"God remembered Noah and all the wild animals and the livestock that were with him in the ark" (v. 8:1).

A dog was once deemed to be the cause of an OU loss.

The university's first mascot was Mex, a tan and white terrier. From 1915-28, Mex could be seen at OU football and baseball games decked out in a red sweater with a big "O" on the side. His major task was to chase away stray dogs during games back in those days "when the football field was more accessible to non-ticketholders." Mex would often clear the field of interlopers even as the Sooners ran a play nearby.

Homeless and abandoned, Mex had been rescued by a U.S. Army field hospital outfit during the Mexican Revolution. One of the soldiers, Mott Keys, took Mex with him when he finished his duty, returned to Oklahoma, and entered the university. Mex landed a home in the Kappa Sigma fraternity house and was soon lauded as the state's most famous dog.

He achieved national fame in 1924 when the OU team took the train north to play Drake on Oct. 25. In Arkansas City, Kan., the players and the boosters switched trains for the final leg to Des Moines and the game. The Sooners were blanked 28-0.

A little detective work uncovered the reason for the loss. In all the excitement, Mex had not changed trains in Arkansas City and had been left behind. A headline in the *Arkansas Daily Traveler* let the world know the whole, sad truth: "Crushing Defeat of Bennie Owen's Team is Charged to Loss of Their Mascot Here."

Somebody scraped up 50 cents as a reward for Mex's return. Three OU grads discovered the dog still in Arkansas City pacing the station platform, and they drove him to the next Sooner game.

Mex died in 1928, and the university closed for his funeral. He was buried in a small casket under Memorial Stadium.

Do you have a dog or two around the place? How about a cat that passes time staring at your caged canary? Kids have gerbils? Maybe you've gone more exotic with a tarantula or a ferret.

We do love our pets; in fact, more households in America have pets than have children. We not only share our living space with animals we love and protect but also with some – such as roaches and rats – that we seek to exterminate.

None of us, though, has ever had to face anything remotely like what Noah did when he packed God's menagerie into one boat. God expressly determined the dimensions of the ark so it could accommodate his creatures. He thus saved all his varmints from extinction, including the fish, the frogs, and the ducks, who must have been quite delighted with the whole flood business.

The lesson is clear for we who strive to live as God would have us: All living things are under God's care. God doesn't call us to care for and respect just our beloved pets; we are to serve God as stewards of all of his creatures.

It's not the size of the dog in the fight but the size of the fight in the dog.
-- Archie Griffin

God cares about all of his creatures,
and he expects us to respect them too.

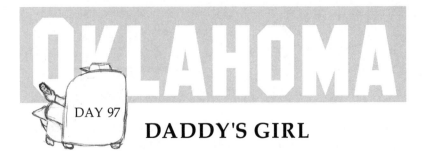

DADDY'S GIRL

Read Luke 3:1-22.

"And a voice came from heaven: 'You are my Son, whom I love; with you I am well pleased'" (v. 22).

Courtney Paris didn't learn much basketball from her father, but he had plenty to teach her about life.

Courtney and her twin sister, Ashley, played for the Sooners from 2005-2009. Courtney is the only player in NCAA history, male or female, to have 700 points, 500 rebounds, and 100 blocks in a season. In 2005-06, she pulled down 539 rebounds, an all-time women's record for a season. She was the first player in U.S. college basketball history with 2,500 points and 2,000 rebounds.

The youngest of eight children (Ashley is older by a scant two minutes.), Courtney received her early instruction on the court from her siblings. Her father was also there for the family games. He is Bubba Paris, who boasts three Super Bowl rings he won as an offensive tackle with the San Francisco 49ers.

He wasn't particularly helpful, though. As Dad admitted, "I was a 20-20-20 man in high school basketball: I played when we were 20 points up, 20 points down or with 20 seconds left." "He was awful at it," Courtney said about her dad's basketball prowess.

But what he lacked on the court, he made up for in life lessons. An evangelist and motivational speaker, Paris Senior taught his children about being born with a God-given purpose. "He said that God knew that [purpose] before we were even thought of,"

Courtney said. "I feel like basketball is my small purpose on Earth. It's something that I can do to share my faith."

Courtney learned Dad's lessons well. She looked for a college that would help her grow as an athlete, a student, and a Christian. Fortunately, that place turned out to be Norman.

Contemporary American society largely belittles and marginalizes fathers and their influence upon their sons and daughters. Men are perceived as necessary to effect pregnancy; after that, they can leave and everybody's better off.

But we need look in only two places to appreciate the enormity of that misconception: our jails – packed with young people who lacked the influence of fathers in their lives as they grew up -- and the Bible. God – being God – could have chosen any relationship he desired between Jesus and himself, including the one society largely extols of irrelevancy.

Instead, the most important relationship in all of history was that of father-son. God obviously believes a close, loving relationship between fathers and sons, such as that of Courtney Paris and her dad, is crucial. For men and women to espouse otherwise or for men to walk blithely and carelessly out of their children's lives constitutes disobedience to the divine will.

Simply put, God loves fathers. After all, he is one.

God has shown me so much favor, and I am just so blessed and happy to be a part of it and work for Him.
-- Courtney Paris on a lesson taught by her father

**Fatherhood is a tough job, but a model
for the father-child relationship is found
in that of Jesus the Son with God the Father.**

DAY 98

THE MOTHER LODE

Read John 19:25-30.

"Near the cross of Jesus stood his mother" (v. 25).

Louis Oubre's momma was clearly in charge of his recruiting process. She even hung up on Bear Bryant.

"I loved to play sports, but I was a little fat boy," Oubre said about growing up in New Orleans. So he played the saxophone in the band. He kept growing, though, until finally in the tenth grade he went out for the team. "I didn't even know how to put on my pads," he recalled. He had to watch everybody else get dressed and imitate what they did.

Oubre almost signed with LSU out of high school. He had a visit scheduled from LSU head coach Charlie McClendon, but Tulane's coaches took him out on a yacht on Lake Pontchartrain and kept him there all day. He missed his appointment.

The Oklahoma coaches actually stumbled onto Oubre accidentally. While they watched a film of a defensive lineman they were considering, this big tackle blocking him caught their attention. It was Oubre. "I am convinced," he said, "that if it wasn't for that game, I wouldn't have gone to Oklahoma."

First, though, the OU coaches had to get past Oubre's mother, the gatekeeper. Fortunately for Sooner football, head coach Barry Switzer sent assistant coach Jerry Pettibone down to New Orleans, and Pettibone immediately hit it off with Oubre's mama.

Bear Bryant, however, wasn't so fortunate. One night about 10, she answered the phone and told the caller, "Louis is in bed; he needs his rest." When the man protested that he was coach Bryant at Alabama and he wanted to speak to her son, she told him, "I don't care who you are. I told you to call back later." Bryant tried to explain some more, but she hung up on him.

Oubre was an All-American tackle and a Sooner team captain in 1980. He was also All-Big Eight in 1979 and '80.

Mamas often do the sort of thing that Louis Oubre's mom did for him: stand watch and protect him when others want something from him. No mother in history, though, has faced a challenge to match that of Mary, whom God chose to be the mother of Jesus. Like mamas and their children throughout time, Mary experienced both joy and perplexity in her relationship with her son.

To the end, though, Mary stood by her boy. She followed him all the way to his execution, an act of love and bravery since Jesus was condemned as an enemy of the Roman Empire.

But just as mothers such as Mary, Louis Oubre's, and perhaps yours would apparently do anything for their children, so will God do anything out of love for his children. After all, that was God on the cross at the foot of which Mary stood, and he was dying for you, one of his children.

My mom [was] running things around the house when it came to recruiting.

— Louis Oubre

Mamas often sacrifice for their children, but God, too, will do anything out of love for his children, including dying on a cross.

DAY 99

CLOTHES HORSE

Read Genesis 37:1-11.

"Israel loved Joseph more than all his children, because he was the son of his old age: and he made him a coat of many colours" (v. 3 KJV).

Merle "Red" Dinkins needed a new sports coat all right, but he needed some underwear worse.

It was said of Dinkins that he "helped America win a war and Bud Wilkinson build a football dynasty." Dinkins was an All-Big Six end in 1944 and then headed off to war. He served in the Pacific, and when hostilities ended, he returned to Norman and played in 1946 for Jim Tatum and in 1947 for Wilkinson.

Dinkins played in an age when the rules regarding money and finances were quite lax. For instance, before the Gator Bowl of Jan. 1, 1947, Tatum asked his players which they would rather have, a watch or $125 cash. The players voted for the money. "I'd give anything now to have the watch," Dinkins later said.

Tatum also set up an arrangement whereby each Sooner player was assigned an Oklahoma City businessman as a "sponsor." The players openly called them their "sugar daddies." The sponsors had access to the players, including the privilege of entering the locker room after games and visiting with them. "Once my sponsor slipped me a twenty-dollar bill," Dinkins said. "I almost fainted. To me it looked as big as a hundred."

At the end of the 1946 season, Dinkins' sponsor phoned him.

"You had a fine year," he said. "Come up to Connolly's and get yourself a new sports coat."

So Dinkins went to the store in Oklahoma City to discover that the going price for a new coat was $125. Somewhat panicked, he called his sponsor. "I need shirts and socks and shorts lots worse than anything else," he said. "Can I substitute them for the sports coat?" The sponsor said okay. Among the items Dinkins bought was his first-ever pair of silk underwear.

Contemporary society proclaims that it's all about the clothes. Buy that new suit or dress, those new shoes, and all the sparkling accessories, and you'll be a new person. The changes are only cosmetic, though; under those clothes, you're the same person. Consider Joseph, for instance, prancing about in his pretty new clothes; he was still a spoiled little tattletale whom his brothers detested enough to sell into slavery.

Jesus never taught that we should run around half-naked or wear only second-hand clothes from the local mission. He did warn us, though, against making consumer items such as clothes a priority in our lives. A follower of Christ seeks to emulate Jesus not through material, superficial means such as wearing special clothing like a robe and sandals. Rather, the disciple desires to match Jesus' inner beauty and serenity -- whether the clothes the Christian wears are the sables of a king or the rags of a pauper.

That's the only time in my life that I ever wore a pair of seven-dollar silk underpants.
-- Merle Dinkins on his shopping spree at Connolly's

Where Jesus is concerned,
clothes don't make the person; faith does.

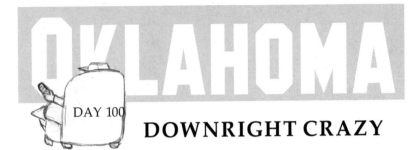

DOWNRIGHT CRAZY

Read Luke 13:31-35.

"Some Pharisees came to Jesus and said to him, 'Leave this place and go somewhere else. Herod wants to kill you.' He replied, 'Go tell that fox . . . I must keep going today and tomorrow and the next day'" (vv. 31-33).

Football players generally don't move willingly from the glamour positions to the offensive line. Chris Chester did, though, and the move turned out to be so shrewd it changed his life.

Chester came to OU as a sure prospect at tight end. Four seasons passed by, however, and he was headed into his last year as the fourth string tight end. He was redshirted in 2001, caught two passes for 25 yards and a touchdown in 2002, and was used sparingly as a blocking tight end in 2003 and 2004.

About the only distinction Chester had gained was head coach Bob Stoops' assertion that his touchdown reception in 2002 was made with his elbows. However Chester caught the ball, it was a big play. It came against Missouri on a fake field goal in the last quarter with OU trailing 24-23 and was the difference in the 31-24 Sooner win.

In the spring of 2005, though, the Sooners found themselves short of offensive linemen. Knowing Chester was an excellent blocker, offensive line coach Kelvin Wilson asked the senior if he would consider sliding down the line. Not surprisingly, Chester was at first reluctant. "It's kind of hard to go from a skill position to the offensive line," he said.

Because the team needed his help and not because he thought it was a smart move, Chester made the switch. He worked hard in the spring, and when the season started, he was the starting right guard. He proved his versatility later in the year by moving again to make three starts at center.

So how did that crazy move pan out? Pretty well. Chester was taken as a guard/center in the second round of the 2006 NFL draft and was a starter in his second season. In 2011, he signed a free agent contract for $20 million. Nothing crazy about that.

What some see as crazy often is shrewd instead. Like the time you went into business for yourself or when you decided to go back to school. Maybe it was when you fixed up that old house. Or when you bought that new company's stock.

You know a good thing when you see it but are also shrewd enough to spot something that's downright crazy. Jesus was that way too. He knew that his entering Jerusalem was in complete defiance of all apparent reason and logic since a whole bunch of folks who wanted to kill him were waiting for him there.

Nevertheless, he went because he also knew that when the great drama had played out he would defeat not only his personal enemies but the most fearsome enemy of all: death itself.

It was, after all, a shrewd move that provided the way to your salvation.

Football is easy if you're crazy.

-- Bo Jackson

It's so good it sounds crazy -- but it's not: through faith in Jesus, you can have eternal life with God.

OKLAHOMA

NOTES
(by Devotion Day Number)

1   When a few students brought . . . fall afternoon in 1895,: J. Brent Clark, *Sooner Century* (Coal Valley, IL: Quality Sports Publications, 1995), p. 28.

1   John A. Harts had played . . . taken place the year before,: Clark, p. 27.

1   few of the 148 university . . . seen an organized contest.: Clark, p. 28.

1   "Let's get up a football team! . . . seat in the local barber shop.: Clark, p. 28.

1   on a field of prairie grass . . . was enrolled in the university.: Clark, pp. 28-29.

1   From Oklahoma City, the . . . but I sure slept good" that night.: Clark, p. 29.

1   Football is all the rage at the university.: Clark, p. 28.

2   "Florida State didn't give us the respect we deserved,": Jeff Snook, *What It Means to Be a Sooner* (Chicago: Triumph Books, 2005), p. 333.

2   "If the oddsmakers decided who won, we'd be 7-4.": Austin Murphy, "Sooner Boomers," Mark Stallard ed., *Echoes of Oklahoma Sooners Football* (Chicago: Triumph Books, 2007), p. 34.

2   "I think they probably . . . big 12 championship game,": Snook, *What It Means to Be a Sooner,* p. 345.

2   "Hey, we have some . . . plan that utterly befuddled": Murphy, "Sooner Boomers," p. 33.

2   the morning of the game . . . "I know it too.": Murphy, "Sooner Boomers," p. 33.

2   The result surprised . . . than anyone else on earth.: Murphy, "Sooner Boomers," p. 34.

3   Soonersports.com unabashedly declares that . . . coach in Big 12 history.: :Athletics: Patty Gasso," *SoonerSports.com,* http://www.soonersports.com/school-bio/patty_gasso.html.

3   and was looking for a new . . . turned into a job offer.: Bobby Anderson, "Boomer Bio: Patty Gasso," *Sooner Spectator Magazine,* Feb. 16, 2006, http://www.soonerspectator.com/featureStory.php?id=97.

3   a Christian who had grown up . . . exhale and move forward.": Joshua Cooley, "Saving the Sooners," *Sharing the Victory,* http://www.sharingthevictory.com/vsItemDisplay.1sp?method=display&objectid=7C71871.

3   It was undeniably what it was supposed to feel like.: Cooley, "Saving the Sooners."

4   "one of the greatest things I ever saw or participated in.": Clark, p. 176.

4   The first time he saw . . . he could land a scholarship.: Snook, *What It Means to Be a Sooner,* p. 224.

4   "What's a scholarship?": Snook, *What It Means to Be a Sooner,* p. 225.

4   "one of the defining moments of Oklahoma football history.": Snook, *What It Means to Be a Sooner,* p. 223.

4   as the crowd chanted . . . led them like a conductor.: Snook, *What It Means to Be a Sooner,* p. 226.

4   Before the game, Hebert . . . the game with a field goal.: Logan Rogers, ""I'll Make Uwe Famous," *BleacherReport.com,* Nov. 4, 2009, http://bleacherreport.com/articles/283868.

4   Hey, the dream's gonna come true.: Rogers, "I'll Make Uwe Famous."

5   he was so far down . . . quarterback the scout team.: Snook, *What It Means to Be a Sooner,* p. 366.

5   The first thing that came . . . "Keep trying.": Snook, *What It Means to Be a Sooner,* p. 368.

5   on June 19th, his 23rd . . . the starter right now.": Snook, *What It Means to Be a Sooner,* p. 368.

5   "Every night of that season . . . that I had stayed.": Snook, *What It Means to Be a Sooner,* p. 369.

6   "with such intangibles as . . . unswerving moral determination.": Booton Herndon, "Bud Wilkinson," Mark Stallard ed., *Echoes of Oklahoma Sooners Football* (Chicago: Triumph Books, 2007), p. 153.

6   Jerry Tubbs was the third-string . . . on the defensive end.: Herndon, "Bud Wilkinson," p. 156.

6   who disliked being dirty . . . were muddy for a game,: Harold Keith, *Forty-Seven Straight* (Norman: University of Oklahoma Press, 2003), p. 16.

6   got right down in the . . . how to do something.": Herndon, "Bud Wilkinson," p. 156.

6   [Bud Wilkinson] believes he . . . knock their heads together.: Herndon, "Bud Wilkinson," p. 149.

7   He wanted to play one more . . . to become a better player.: Kelli Anderson, "Post Impressionist," *Sports Illustrated,* Jan. 26, 2009, http://sportsillustrated.cnn.com/vault/article/magazine/MAG1150929/index.htm.

7   "two strong Christian role models . . . to not leave anything behind.": Nick Dunn, "Above All Else," *FCA.org,* March 16, 2009, http://www.fca.org/vsItemDisplay.1sp?objectID=4CE3B38A.

7   That's one of the things . . . it's supposed to be played.: Dunn, "Above All Else."

8   "Although the sun was shining brightly, it was raining.": Clark, p. 126.

8   "We wanted to beat everybody 40-zip,": Clark, pp. 126-27.

8   UCLA's head coach had tabbed them "the greatest team of the era.": Clark, p. 127.

8   He ordered quarterback Jimmy . . . getting up off the ground,": Clark, p. 127.

SOONERS

8   Get out of the way! Here they come again!: Clark, p. 127.

9   "a cauldron of noise and pressure,": Pat Forde, "Landry Jones' Maturity on Full Display," *ESPN. com*, Sept. 17, 2011, http://espn.go.com/college-football/story/_/id6988141.

9   "Doak [Campbell Stadium] was . . . had seen this movie before.": Forde, "Landry Jones' Maturity."

9   "a steely display of poise, power and playmaking.": Forde, "Landry Jones' Maturity."

9   the offense "muscled up and pounded out": Forde, "Landry Jones' Maturity."

9   Bob Stoops called the best . . . fourth quarter since 2000.: Forde, "Landry Jones' Maturity."

9   They sense blood, the . . . we just seized it right back.: Forde, "Landry Jones' Maturity."

10 he wanted his team to look . . . toss onto the ground.: Jeff Snook, *"Then Bud Said to Barry Who Told Bob . . ."* (Chicago: Triumph Books, 2008), p. 21.

10 the game was generally regarded . . . just to keep focused,": Snook, *"Then Bud Said to Barry,*" p. 22.

10 He never did settle down, . . . excited on the sideline," Snook, *"Then Bud Said to Barry,*" p. 23.

10 The intense head coach wanted . . . about lost his marbles.": Snook, *"Then Bud Said to Barry,*" p. 23.

11 He was the first OU freshman . . . of an indomitable spirit": Bob Hersom, "Resler Is Inspiring Force on OU Line," *The Oklahoman*, Sept. 19, 1991, http://newsok.com/article/2369386.

11 He played baseball until junior . . . his shirts with snaps.: Richard Hoffer, "Big Man on Campus," *Sports Illustrated*, Sept. 28, 1992, http://sportsillustrated.cnn.com/vault/article/magazine/ MAG1004272/index.htm.

11 It's amazing what he . . . on the first play.: Hersom, "Resler Is Inspiring Force."

11 It never occurred to me that I couldn't.: Hoffer, "Big Man on Campus."

12 Circumstances forced Coale to change . . . aren't affected by difficulties.: Jenni Carlson, "Sherri Coale Sets Tough Mindset for Sooners," *The Oklahoman*, March 19, 2012, http://newsok.com/ ou-womens-basketball.

12 Tough teams find a way . . . that for the most part.: Carlson, "Sherri Coale Sets Tough Mindset."

13 Bryan missed out on . . . years older than me.": Snook, *What It Means to Be a Sooner*, pp. 283-84.

13 "I figured I would . . . the great Oklahoma Sooners,": Snook, *What It Means to Be a Sooner*, p. 285.

13 Bryan left home in August . . . the strength to survive.": Snook, *What It Means to Be a Sooner*, p. 287.

13 I was scared, I was homesick, and I was lost.: Snook, *What It Means to Be a Sooner*, p. 287.

14 With 3:50 to play in the . . . the rabid OU fans obeyed them.: Keith, p. 231.

14 When the game ended, PA . . . that was pretty classy,": Snook, *What It Means to Be a Sooner*, p. 88.

14 The following Monday, at . . . all the way through forty-seven.: Keith, p. 232.

14 They were strictly big league about it.: Keith, p. 232.

15 Defensive coordinator Brent Venables started . . . they would do, they did.": Austin Murphy, "Take That, Texas!" *Sports Illustrated*, Dec. 1, 2008, http://sportsillustrated.cnn.com/vault/article/ magazine/MAG1149149/index.html.

15 "the Red Raiders were . . . world of hurt awaiting them.": Murphy, "Take That, Texas!"

15 "When you manhandle someone," . . . it wanted from Tech.": Murphy, "Take That, Texas!"

15 Last year in Lubbock, . . . be the more physical team.: Murphy, "Take That, Texas!"

16 We didn't have any superstars,": "Baseball: NCAA Tournament History: 1994 National Champions," *SoonerSports.com*, http://www.soonersports.com/sports/m-basebl/archive/94-national-champs.html.

16 "We got hot at the right time.": "Baseball: NCAA Tournament History: 1994 National Champions."

16 trailed in only one of . . . the entire NCAA Tournament.: "Baseball: NCAA Tournament History: 1994 National Champions."

16 "The momentum that we got in Austin carried over,": "Baseball: NCAA Tournament History: 1994 National Champions."

16 "This was a team in the . . . did what it took to win.": "Baseball: NCAA Tournament History: 1994 National Champions."

16 Twenty-five guys pulling on the same rope.: "Baseball: NCAA Tournament History: 1994 National Champions."

17 Humpty Dumpty, Whoop to do; What's the matter with Okla. U.?": Clark, p. 33.

17 In the fall of 1898, pioneering . . . Norman lads to a 5-0 win.; Clark, p. 31.

17 After the game, the players . . . wash away the grime from the game.": Clark, pp. 31-32.

17 When the triumphant players . . . the crowd with clever yells.": Clark, p. 32.

17 An Oklahoma yell card from 1910, . . . Boomer! Sooner! Oklahoma U!": Clark, p. 33.

17 Riff, raff, Riff, raff, ruff. We play football and never get enough.: Clark, p. 33.

18 "Throughout the Oklahoma football . . . Not even for the night games.: Carter Strickland, "Just a Little Something to Believe In," *The Oklahoman*, Oct. 15, 2004, p. 1C.

18 We're a superstitious team.: Strickland, "Just a Little Something to Believe In."

19 "Smoke through a keyhole.": Clark, p. 171.

19 he "held the franchise on Sooner excitement.": Clark, p. 171.

19   Prior to the 1972 Colorado . . . they won't have time.": Snook, *Then Bud Said to Barry*, pp. 124-25.
19   In the film room after the . . . silver shoes in high school,: Snook, *"Then Bud Said to Barry*, p. 125.
19   I don't care if he plays barefoot. Just give him the ball.: Snook, *"Then Bud Said to Barry*, p. 126.
20   Three weeks before Kelley's . . . because it seems like it's normal.": Jenni Carlson, "Giant Leaps, No
      Bounds," *The Oklahoman*, March 2, 2010, http://newsok.com/jenni-carlson-giant-leaps-no-
      bounds-for-ou-gymnast/article/3443170.
20   I've always been pretty good with pain.: Carlson, "Giant Leaps, No Bounds."
21   "Considered one of . . . players in Sooners history,": Snook, *What It Means to Be a Sooner*, p. 23.
21   Royal's father took the family . . . to play football for OU.: Snook, *What It Means to Be a Sooner*, p. 18.
21   When his high school football . . . could catch a ride.: Snook, *What It Means to Be a Sooner*, p. 19.
21   All these years, I wished . . . thank him for his kindness.: Snook, *What It Means to Be a Sooner*, p. 19.
22   "Intimidation," was the way . . . described what happened.: Roy S. Johnson, "Oklahoma Rallies,"
      Mark Stallard ed., *Echoes of Oklahoma Sooners Football* (Chicago: Triumph Books, 2007), p. 32.
22   what head coach Barry Switzer referred to as "a great test.": Johnson, "Oklahoma Rallies," p. 32.
22   Jackson made a one-handed grab: Johnson, "Oklahoma Rallies," p. 32.
22   We've done it so many times . . . can win any ballgame.: Johnson, "Oklahoma Rallies," p. 31.
23   "Please, dear Lord, don't let the best team win.": Clark, p. 175.
23   "that day at Lincoln, OU seemed outmanned.": Clark, p. 175.
24   The genial Texan early on . . . try to feed them God.": David Pond, "Sooner or Later," *Sharing the
      Victory*, Dec. 2009, http://www.sharingthevictory.com/vsItemDisplay.1sp?method=display&
      objectid=4356375.
24   For the first time in her . . . started becoming uplifting,": Pond, "Sooner or Later."
25   he even had a poster of . . . OU's guest for the 2003 Texas game.: Austin Murphy, "The Oklahoma
      Kid," *Sports Illustrated*, Oct. 11, 2004, http://sportsillustrated.cnn.com/vault/article/magazine/
      MAG1105800/index.htm.
26   Bennie Owen's obsession was speed,: Clark, p. 62.
26   He had landed his nickname . . . Because Geyer could hit the spot,: "Football: All-American: Forest
      'Spot' Geyer," *SoonerSports.com*, http://www.soonersports.com/sports/m-footbl/archive/aa-
      forest-geyer-1915.html.
26   "was successfully slinging the ball . . . such as the Nebraska Cornhuskers.": Clark, p. 64.
26   Geyer operated as a halfback out of a deep punt formation.: Clark, p. 66.
26   Geyer always had the option of faking the run and then throwing on the run.: Clark, p. 66.
26   Oklahoma was the first team in America to rely on the forward pass.: Clark, p. 71.
27   The junior-college QB had one . . . "Yes, we could.": George Schroeder & Berry Tramel, "A Season
      to Shout About," *No 1 Better* (Oklahoma City: *The Oklahoman*, 2001), p. 9.
27   The answer didn't impress . . . believed what he said.: George Schroeder, "Heupel's Dream in Au-
      gust Became Reality in January," *No 1 Better* (Oklahoma City: *The Oklahoman*, 2001), p. 106.
27   Almost two years later, on . . . His eyes misted.": Schroeder, "Heupel's Dream," p. 104.
27   Before the season started, . . . the whole season started,": Schroeder, "Heupel's Dream," p. 104.
27   You could tell he really . . . that we could get there.: Schroeder, "Heupel's Dream," p. 106.
28   Just under 12,000 fans . . . all the seats were taken.: George Schroeder, "Big Crowd Gives OU Lift,"
      The Oklahoman, Feb. 5, 2007, p. 20B.
28   State head coach Kurt Budke . . . every bit of that tonight.": Schroeder, "Big Crowd."
28   characterized as "sloppy and sluggish." John Helsley, "Sooners Catch Fire, Beat OSU," *The Oklaho-
      man*, Feb. 5, 2007, p. 20B.
28   falling behind 25-16 ten minutes into the game.: Schroeder, "Big Crowd."
28   Coale stood up on the . . . players on the floor: Fight!": Helsley, "Sooners Catch Fire."
28   We have got to get used to executing when the crowd gets loud.: Schroeder, "Big Crowd."
29   Owens' brothers drove the future . . . were at a mental institution.: Snook, *What It Means to Be a
      Sooner*, pp. 125-26.
29   Owens called his dad and told . . . to stay in Norman.": Snook, *What It Means to Be a Sooner*, p. 126.
29   He simply found a first-team . . . He was a starter.: Snook, *What It Means to Be a Sooner*, p. 127.
29   He was to sit by the phone . . . how he got the news.: Snook, *What It Means to Be a Sooner*, p. 128.
29   Did the boy win that there trophy?: Snook, *What It Means to Be a Sooner*, p. 128.
30   The Monday morning after OU's . . . come back and watch him,": Jenni Carlson, "Oklahoma's
      Frank Alexander," *The Oklahoman*, Oct, 12, 2011, p. 1C.
30   "It can't get any better, to tell you the truth,": Carlson, "Oklahoma's Frank Alexander."
30   He could've died. . . . just been a blessing.: Carlson, "Oklahoma's Frank Alexander."
31   they were the self-appointed . . . the local question: Why?": Jay C. Upchurch, *Tales from the Sooners
      Sideline* (Champaign, IL: Sports Publishing L.L.C., 2007), p. 92.
31   the player explained that . . . taken him down to the bus station.: Upchurch, pp. 92-93.

31   uncovering some clues as to . . . all that needed to be said.": Upchurch, p. 93.

32   "Living a Christ-like life . . . whenever there's a challenge.": Mark Palmer, "Christian Faith Serves Wrestlers," *Intermat*, Aug. 14, 2009, http://www.intermatwrestle.coom/articles/5357.

32   a short time after his loss, . . . room and back to practice.: Andrew Gillman, "OU's Hazewinkel Vows to Work at NCAAs," *The Oklahoman*, March 16, 2005, p. 1C.

32   I'm not out there wrestling for myself. I'm wrestling for the Lord.: Palmer, "Christian Faith."

33   Lofton had his doubters . . . with his physical ability,": Scott Wright, "OU Football: 18 Tackles, Touchdown," *The Oklahoman*, Oct. 16, 2007, p. 1C.

33   their spread offense that . . . attempting open-field tackles.: Wright, "OU Football."

33   defensive coordinator Brent Venables called "outstanding,": Wright, "OU Football."

33   When Venables saw the play . . . and scooped and scored.": Wright, "OU Football."

34   When Bennie Owen came to . . . seated five hundred spectators.: Clark, p. 45.

34   with a three-month contract for $900.: Clark, p. 45.

34   "Nowhere in America was there . . . creative football mind" than Owen.: Clark, p. 57.

34   Who can Oklahoma play next? All southwestern teams are outclassed.: Clark, p. 62.

35   As a freshman in 1976, Watts was the Sooners' seventh-string quarterback.": "J.C. Watts," *Wikipedia, the free encyclopedia*. http://en.wikipedia.org/wiki/J._C._Watts.

35   "My first months in . . . decided to stick around,": Snook, *What It Means to Be a Sooner*, p. 257.

35   Because you fail doesn't make you a failure.: Snook, *What It Means to Be a Sooner*, p. 259.

36   They were tumultuous years, . . . halftime of the '34 Tulane game.: Upchurch, p. 11.

36   "He kind of ran the football team . . . posted it on a bulletin board.: Upchurch, p. 12.

36   At the end of Jones' first . . . basically in your throat,": Upchurch, p. 12.

36   It was pretty scary walking up and looking at that list.: Upchurch, p. 12.

37   "Anytime I sit on the bench, . . . like to do eventually,": Kelli Anderson, "Price Is Right," *Sports Illustrated*, Jan. 21, 2002, http://sportsillustrated.cnn.com/vault/article/magazine/ MAG1024800/index.htm.

37   "one of the best and most beloved Sooners.": George Schroeder, "Hollis Price: Heartfelt Desire," *The Oklahoman*, Aug. 31, 2005, http://newsok.com/hollis-price.

37   He played much of his . . . made me focus more.": Anderson, Price Is Right."

37   He grew up in New Orleans' . . . one of the chosen ones,": Schroeder, "Hollis Price."

37   He's not a big, strong kid, but mentally he's as tough as they come.: Anderson, "Price Is Right."

38   It included the spread offense, . . . that should expect championships.": Schroeder & Tramel, "A Season to Shout About," p. 11.

38   Safety Ontei Jones said . . . going to work.": Schroeder & Tramel, "A Season to Shout About," p. 11.

38   "We never had a date . . . sooner than later.": Schroeder & Tramel, "A Season to Shout About," p. 11.

38   I had some ideas . . . you can every day.: Schroeder & Tramel, "A Season to Shout About," p. 11.

39   OU's football program was "floundering . . . old and dusty.": Snook, *"Then Bud Said to Barry*, p. 12.

39   He realized that the . . . that Oklahoma can be proud of.": Snook, *"Then Bud Said to Barry*, p. 11.

39   he insisted that the new coach . . . A miffed Tatum complied,: Snook, *"Then Bud Said to Barry*, p. 13.

39   We want to build a . . . football team can be proud of.: Snook, *"Then Bud Said to Barry*, p. 14.

40   In the summer of 1969, Sooner . . . the shot impressive distances.: Upchurch, p. 79.

40   Martin introduced himself and . . . whipping his All-Americas.: Upchurch, p. 80.

40   That's unheard of. A walk-on . . . Derland [Moore] was the real deal.: Upchurch, p. 81.

41   Two things were solid in Jones' world: her soccer and her faith.: Bob Schaller, *Faith of the Sooners* (Grand Island, NE: Cross Training Publishing, 2002), p. 7.

41   In 2000, though, that began . . . God off to the side,": Schaller, *Faith of the Sooners*, p. 8.

41   One horrible night spring . . . in August.' I wasn't.": Schaller, *Faith of the Sooners*, pp. 8-9.

41   The team trainer held a Bible . . . and off the soccer team,: Schaller, *Faith of the Sooners*, p. 10.

41   "Whoever turned me in . . . lead me back to Christ,": Schaller, *Faith of the Sooners*, p. 11.

41   in 2002, one goalie was injured and the other studied abroad.: Schaller, *Faith of the Sooners*, p. 12.

41   She was born with a cataract . . . legally blind in that eye.: Schaller, *Faith of the Sooners*, p. 12.

41   the one-eyed goalie . . . because of her renewed faith.: Schaller, *Faith of the Sooners*, p. 13.

41   You can believe what you . . . peace in her life.: Schaller, *Faith of the Sooners*, p. 10.

42   Even while Broyles was . . . mission trip to Haiti.: Thayer Evans, "Broyles' Playbook Now the Good Book," *FoxSports.com*, Sept. 17, 2011,http://msn.foxsports.com/collegefootball/story.

42   Ryan has grown . . . looking for in a leader.": Evans, "Broyles' Playbook Now the Good Book."

43   In the locker room before . . . got big all of a sudden,": Clark, p. 173.

43   Hold your heads up. You are a great ballclub.: Clark, p. 172.

44   Each player had to find . . . onto the field in the middle of play.: Clark, p. 30.

44   when the Logan County sheriff . . . engaged in a newfangled game.: Clark, p. 31.

44   I was feeling kind of blue, but I had liked the rough physical contact.: Clark, p. 29.

45   "She was definitely one of the best out there,": Paul Putignano, "The Emotions of

OKLAHOMA

Sports: From a Low to a High," *the-signal.com*. Aug. 6, 2011. http://www.the-signal.com/archives/49133.

45   As the season wore on . . . playing the game she loved.: Putignano, "The Emotions of Sports."
45   I forgot how much fun it is to play this game.: Putignano, "The Emotions of Sports."
46   "the finest option quarterback in OU history": Snook, *What It Means to Be a Sooner*, p. 211.
46   Once, though, Lott asked head coach . . . I tied mine up in the front.": Berry Tramel, "Switzer Tales: Washington's Silver Shoes, Lott's Bandana," *Berry Tramel's Blog*, May 13, 2010, http://blog. news.ok.com/berrytramel/2010/05/13.
46   He told himself that he . . . of his sophomore season.: Snook, *What It Means to Be a Sooner*, p. 214.
46   In that fourth game, . . . following game against Texas.: Snook, *What It Means to Be a Sooner*, p. 215.
46   I had been named . . . of my self-imposed deadline.: Snook, *What It Means to Be a Sooner*, p. 215.
47   "maybe the single most revered play in Sooners history.": Jake Trotter, "10 Seasons Ago, 'Superman' took Flight," *ESPN.com*, Oct. 6, 2011, http://espn.go.com/colleges/oklahoma/football/story/_/id/7065608.
47   OU led 7-3 early in the . . . "Don't leave your feet!": Austin Murphy, "Boomer Sooner," *Sports Illustrated*, Oct. 15, 2001, http://sportsillustrated.cnn.com/vault/article/magazine/MAG1023973/index.htm.
47   It felt like I was in the air forever.: Trotter, "10 Seasons Ago."
48   Rhodes had narrowed his choices . . . the heck was going on.: Upchurch, p. 115.
48   later that night, the passengers . . . a few weeks later.: Upchurch, p. 116.
48   [The sailor] basically recruited Steve to OU for us.: Upchurch, p. 116.
49   Sometimes pride and effort are all you have.": Berry Tramel, "The Gospel of Sampson," *The Oklahoman*, March 12, 2004, p. 13C.
49   Senior forward Johnnie Gilbert . . . booted off the team.: Tramel, "The Gospel of Sampson."
49   "the ball bounced everywhere but into the Sooners' basket.": George Schroeder, "Back from the Brink," *The Oklahoman*, March 12, 2004, p. 1C.
49   head coach Kelvin Sampson preached . . . badges of honor.": Tramel, "The Gospel of Sampson."
49   "In the second half, we . . . would take care of itself.": Schroeder, "Back from the Brink."
49   Part of a 10-0 run . . . lead with 12:18 left.: Schroeder, "Back from the Brink."
49   A lot of players on this team do have a lot of pride.: Tramel, "The Gospel of Sampson."
50   "Last year was a big disaster,": Jake Trotter, "Back Where He Belongs," *The Oklahoman*, Oct. 12, 2010, p. 3C.
50   He struggled with the new . . . made it on the field.: Trotter, "Back Where He Belongs."
50   "It was a learning process . . . for what I want.": Trotter, "Back Where He Belongs."
50   "I'm loving it," . . . after the 28-20 win over Texas.: Trotter, "Back Where He Belongs."
50   When he is in there, you feel good about it.: Trotter, "Back Where He Belongs."
50   he may well have been . . . with that innovation in 1941.: Snook, *What It Means to Be a Sooner*, p. 14.
51   He was the first . . . make the varsity football team.: Snook, *What It Means to Be a Sooner*, p. 9.
51   he also contracted pneumatic . . . through high school.: Snook, *What It Means to Be a Sooner*, p. 10.
51   It kind of got to be a thing . . . a circus act or something.: Snook, *What It Means to Be a Sooner*, p. 10.
52   Barry Switzer felt the 28-27 . . . had to make another change.: Clark, p. 154.
52   Switzer had prevously talked to . . . switch to the wishbone.: Upchurch, p. 91.
52   "the most significant and gutsy move in OU's football history.": "Football: Head Coaches: Barry Switzer (1973-1988)," *SoonerSports.com*, http://www.soonersports.com/sports-m-footbl/archive/head_coaches.html.
52   the change saved the coaches' . . . "Oklahoma's second football dynasty.": "Football: Head Coaches: Barry Switzer (1973-1988)."
52   To change in the middle . . . it hard to fathom why.: Upchurch, p. 92.
53   contest was dubbed "The Perfect Game.": *The Road to No. 1* (Chicago, Triumph Books, 2003), p. 46.
53   "We didn't want to get 80," . . . what we wanted to do,": *The Road to No. 1*, p. 47.
53   "You don't expect this,": *The Road to No. 1*, p. 46.
53   The game ended with a handoff . . . best team in the nation,": *The Road to No. 1*, p. 47.
54   "A lot players overseas after . . . playing for OU. It's incredible,": Will Estel, "Oklahoma Student Athlete Spotlight: Jelena Cerina," *Big12Sports.com*, Feb. 15, 2012, http://www.big12sports.com/ViewArticle.dbml?DB_OEM_ID=10410&ATCLID=205379.
54   We never heard anything about colleges.: Estel, "Oklahoma Student Athlete Spotlight."
55   SI's official proclamation came . . . college football's biggest prize.: Albert Chen, "A Punishing Run," *Sports Illustrated*, Dec. 15, 2008, http://sportsillustrated.cnn.com/vault/article/magazine/MAG1149625/index.html.
55   The team set a major . . . scoring team in the country.: Chen, "A Punishing Run."
55   "what has turned Oklahoma into . . . running again at full speed.: Chen, "A Punishing Run."

56   When Vessels was 14, . . . to play for the Sooners.: "Billy Vessels (1931-2001," *Encyclopedia of Okla-homa History & Culture*, http://digital.library.okstate.edu/encyclopedia/entries/V/VE005.html.
56   spending the summer of . . . the hot, dry river sand,: Clark, p. 120.
56   the first football game to be televised nationally,: "Billy Vessels (1931-2001)."
57   When the Sooners beat . . . on the practice field within days.: Clark, p. 50.
57   Newcomer Charley Wantland reported . . . not protective equipment,": Clark, p. 49.
57   disdaining gear such as helmets because it slowed his players down.: Clark, p. 62.
58   Against Texas Tech on Feb. 16, . . . to freshman Tony Neysmith.: Scott Wright, "No Doghouse for Sooners' Godbold," *The Oklahoman*, 17 Feb. 2008, p. 1B.
58   Godbold had angered head . . . us to another level," Wright, "No Doghouse for Sooners' Godbold."
58   The doghouse is where you sit on the end of the bench and don't play.: Wright, "No Doghouse."
59   But an OU lineman . . . for an illegal substitution.: Upchurch, *Tales from the Sooners Sideline*, p. 127.
59   As soon as Lashar's kick . . . unsportsmanlike conduct penalty.: Jenni Carlson, "Driver Recalls the Schooner Slipup," *The Oklahoman*, Sept. 8, 2006, p. 1A.
59   "The wheels pretty much came off for us after that,": Upchurch, *Tales from the Sooners Sideline*, p. 127.
59   The whole thing was . . . it all played out.: Upchurch, *Tales from the Sooners Sideline*, p. 127.
60   He wanted to play for the best: G. Neri, "Wahoo! The Incredible Adventures of Chief Wahoo McDaniel," *HungerMountain.org*, July 31, 2009, http://www.hungermtn.org/wahoo.
60   he won $185 when some . . . like an old pickup truck.": Mike Shropshire, "Wahoo McDaniel," *Sports Illustrated*, July 2, 2001, http://sportsillustrated.cnn.com/vault/article/magazine/MAG1022918/index.htm.
61   OU played Nebraska that year with fewer than fifty scholarship athletes available.: Clark, p. 201
61   With Oklahoma trailing 14-7 late . . . half ended for a second time.: Clark, p. 206.
62   "one of the most interesting, . . . and scribble it down.: Clark, p. 100.
62   before the season was over, . . . interview for the Maryland job.; Clark, p. 102.
62   "an atmosphere of enthusiasm and an inventory of young talent.": Clark, p. 103.
62   "We do not choose whether . . . on which we will stand.": R. Alan Culpepper, "The Gospel of Luke: Introduction, Commentary, and Reflections," *The New Interpreter's Bible*, Vol. IX (Nashville: Abingdon Press, 1998), p. 153.
63   You just wait and see." . . . he wasn't good enough.: Snook, *What It Means to Be a Sooner*, p. 242.
63   Cumby actually played . . I could breathe again.": Snook, *What It Means to Be a Sooner*, pp. 238-39.
63   He planned to go . . . College after graduation,: Snook, *What It Means to Be a Sooner*, p. 240.
63   One day, though, he was . . . never make it up there.": Snook, *What It Means to Be a Sooner*, p. 241.
63   An uncle had told him . . . determined not to fail.: Snook, *What It Means to Be a Sooner*, p. 242.
63   There was no way I . . . superintendent had told me.: Snook, *What It Means to Be a Sooner*, p. 242.
64   When the Oklahoma baseball team . . . the 2010 College World Series.: John Helsley, "Rocha Worked His Way Back into Sooner Rotation," *The Oklahoman*, May 19, 2011, p. 5C.
64   It was like, 'Maybe . . . to play me anymore': Helsley, "Rocha Worked His Way Back."
65   "Dang!" What's up with that?": George Schroeder, "Griffin Scores 6 TD's Against UT," *No 1 Better* (Oklahoma City: The Oklahoman, 2001), p. 38.
65   "more than what I expected.": Schroeder, "Griffin Scores 6 TD's," p. 40.
66   UT head coach Mack . . . scoreboard in the background.: Schroeder, "Griffin Scores 6 TD's," p. 40.
66   Young was still practicing for . . . juggling a trio of oranges.: "Waddy Young," *Wikipedia, the free encyclopedia*, http://en.wikipedia.org/wiki/Waddy_Young.
66   Young flew more than 9,000 combat hours: Berry Tramel, "Young a War Hero, Kind Man," *The Oklahoman*, Aug. 30, 2007, http://news.ok.com.
66   After the war in Europe . . . new B-29 Super Fortresses.: "Waddy Young," *Wikipedia*.
66   On Jan. 9, 1945, Young was . . . was "We are OK.": Tramel, "Young a War Hero."
67   "hard by the banks of the rain-swollen Cottonwood Creek.": Clark, p. 40.
67   The game was played in harsh, . . . on the OU team had a touchdown: Clark, p. 41.
68   Following the 1989-90 . . . in her hands sobbing.: Austin Murphy, "Back from the Dead," *Sports Illustrated*, March 18, 2002, http://sportsillustrated.cnn.com/vault/article/magazine/MAG1025163/index.htm.
68   If you coach for 25 years . . . for Christ, that is success.: Susie Magill, "'Coales' of Wisdom." *Sharing the Victory*, March 2009, http://www.sharingthevictory.com/vsItemDisplay.1sp?method=display&objectid=09AC87.
69   Many historians still consider . . . the finest in OU history.: Clark, p. 166.
69   *Sports Illustrated* called the Sooners "The Best Team You'll Never See.": Clark, p. 167.
69   "OU's most suffocating defense ever." . . . act in college football history.": Clark, p. 166.
69   They grew up in grinding poverty . . . to keep his mouth shut.: John Underwood,

"Oklahomans Call It Selmonizing," *Sports Illustrated*, Nov. 12, 1973, http://sportsillustrated. cnn.com/vault/article/magazine/MAG1087997/index.htm.

69 God Bless Mrs. Selmon!: Clark, p. 166.

70 He landed hard on that . . . then dropped to his knees.: Damon Hack, "A Shoulder to Lean On.," *Sports Illustrated*, April 26, 2010, http://sportsillustrated.cnn.com/vault/article/magazine/ MAG1168636/index.htm.

70 It was the longest he . . . family and friends continually,: Hack, "A Shoulder to Lean On."

70 His workouts started immediately . . . His shoulder held up,: Hack, "A Shoulder to Lean On."

70 If I'd just tried to . . . more pressure on my shoulder.: Hack, "A Shoulder to Lean On."

71 Wilkinson knew it was . . . what would come his way.: Snook, *Then Bud Said to Barry*, p. 69.

71 "Either Coach Wilkinson was . . . or he was very lucky.": Snook, *Then Bud Said to Barry*, p. 69.

71 "In many ways," . . . and school and teammates.": Snook, *Then Bud Said to Barry*, p. 70.

71 On the day of its dedication, . . . running down our cheeks.": Snook, *Then Bud Said to Barry*, p. 71.

71 "He had more class . . . he was a better student,": Snook, *Then Bud Said to Barry*, p. 72.

71 It was the most significant thing I did when I was coaching.: Snook, *Then Bud Said to Barry*, p. 72.

72 "When Jack Frost was nipping . . . the dean's list next semester: Hank Hersch, "King Reigns," *Sports Illustrated*, Nov. 25, 1992, http://sportsillustrated.cnn.com/vault/article/magazine/ MAG1141563/index.htm.

72 We didn't have a Leave It to Beaver-type conversation.: Hersch, "King Reigns."

73 The 2009 was to be the . . . chance to get out there.": Mike Baldwin, "Patience Pays Off for DE Macon," *The Oklahoman*, Oct. 14, 2010, pp. 1C, 4C.

73 Making it harder for Macon . . . he had ever coached.: Jake Trotter, "Decision to Stick It Out Paying Off," *The Oklahoman*, Dec. 27, 2010, http://newsok.com/decision-to-stick-it-out.

73 "one of the best single- . . . of the Bob Stoops era.": Trotter, "Decision to Stick It Out Paying Off."

73 "God had a plan for me," . . . out and kept fighting.": Trotter, "Decision to Stick It Out Paying Off."

73 Pryce [Macon] is a good example of perseverance.: Baldwin, "Patience Pays Off for DE Macon."

74 "the only player in the . . . when he was a freshman.": Snook, *Then Bud Said to Barry*, p. 87.

74 On the practice field at . . . sat down on a bench.: Snook, *Then Bud Said to Barry*, p. 88.

74 "He had mud all over him . . . to appear very tired.": Snook, *Then Bud Said to Barry*, pp. 88-89.

74 The coaches walked in and . . . a Sooner practice-field legend.: Snook, *Then Bud Said to Barry*, p. 89.

74 We were all amazed, . . . died laughing right there.: Snook, *Then Bud Said to Barry*, p. 88.

75 Lundegreen was well on . . . God wanted him to be.: Schaller, *Faith of the Sooners*, p. 144.

75 The dream literally came . . . a spotlight shined on him.: Schaller, *Faith of the Sooners*, p. 145.

75 Before his sophomore season, . . . of running him over.: Schaller, *Faith of the Sooners*, p. 140.

75 Lundegreen dived for the side . . . he ran one guy down.": Schaller, *Faith of the Sooners*, p. 141.

75 I had to drive two . . . with the busted ankle.: Schaller, *Faith of the Sooners*, p. 141.

76 One night during his junior . . . and two Texas tickets.: Berry Tramel, "Daryl Hunt: An OU Football Star of Substance," *Berry Tramel's Blog*, July 14, 2010, http://blog.newsok.com/berrytramel/ 2010/07/14.

76 The interest that [Daryl] Hunt . . . we should live our lives.: Tramel, "Daryl Hunt."

77 Following the '52 season, Roberts was . . . "Just come sit on our bench.": Snook, *What It Means to Be a Sooner*, p. 45.

77 Head coach Bud Wilkinson had his . . . for interrogating him so.: Snook, *What It Means to Be a Sooner*, p. 46.

78 "It happened so quickly," . . . We've got to buckle up.'": George Schroeder, "Sooners Conquer No. 1 Nebraska," *No 1 Better* (Oklahoma City: *The Oklahoman*, 2001), p. 50.

78 the players and coaches said . . . about the sudden deficit.: Schroeder, "Sooners Conquer No. 1 Nebraska," p. 53.

78 No one panicked. . . . had to get settled in.: Schroeder, "Sooners Conquer No. 1 Nebraska," p. 53.

79 The two Sooners hopped in . . . one foot of the pin: "OU Golf Spotlight: Walter Emery," *Sooner Sports.com*, Sept. 14, 2009. http://www.soonersports.com/sports/m-golf/spec-rel/091409aaa. html.

79 I'd make a good iron . . . Nobody said anything.: "OU Golf Spotlight: Walter Emery."

80 "Switzer and his Sooners were at their best when their backs were against the wall.": Clark, p. 161.

80 The Cowboys led 20-3 with ten . . . he eluded two defenders: Clark, p. 185.

80 At first, he ordered an onside . . . Scott Case at the Cowboy 49.: Clark, p. 186.

80 this was the longest field goal of his Sooner career.: Clark, p. 186.

81 "epic Bedlam.": George Schroeder, "Classic," *The Oklahoman*, Oct. 31, 2004, p. 1C.

81 When Bradley arrived in . . . of his athletic ability,": George Schroeder, "OU's Bradley Hits His Stride," *The Oklahoman*, Nov. 5, 2004, p. 5C.

81 when White hit him on . . . gathered the ball in.: Schroeder, "OU's Bradley Hits His Stride."

81   It was just perfect.: Schroeder, "OU's Bradley Hits His Stride."

82   He played football as a . . . senior safety, wingback, and punter.: Snook, *What It Means to Be a Sooner*, p. 179.

82   At the time, the freshmen . . . the varsity in practice.: Snook, *What It Means to Be a Sooner*, p. 180.

82   That earned him a promotion . . . your fears dissipate.: Snook, *What It Means to Be a Sooner*, p. 181.

82   I wasn't jawing back . . . to death of an opponent.: Snook, *What It Means to Be a Sooner*, p. 181.

83   tackle Wade Walker was knocked . . . wandering into the Longhorn huddle.: Keith, p. 61.

83   Wilkinson had his team hole . . . any connection to the trio.: Keith, p. 69.

83   It didn't fire us up. We were ready to play anyhow.: Keith, p. 69.

84   Each year while she was . . . "It's a dream.": Jenni Carlson, "Love Was in the Air for Stewart," *The Oklahoman*, May 30, 2000, http://newsok.com/article/2699282.

84   she didn't really think she . . . Give me the ball.": Carlson, "Love Was in the Air."

84   "Who could've written it this way?" . . . that dominated women's softball.: Carlson, "Love Was in the Air."

84   "I can't believe it,": Carlson, "Love Was in the Air."

84   Every kid dreams of being a part of this game.: Carlson, "Love Was in the Air."

85   "I just felt at the time . . . game back in our hands.: *The Road to No. 1*, p. 16.

85   "they had no prayer of stopping . . . how else to explain it.": *The Road to No. 1*, p. 18.

85   "I saw them come out with the fake punt (call), and I could not believe it,": *The Road to No. 1*, p. 18.

85   To head coach Bob Stoops, it's just another play.: *The Road to No. 1*, p. 18.

86   this bespectacled English professor. . . . Territory and its university.": Clark, p. 24.

86   Students then formed a team . . . against Norman High School.: Clark, p. 29.

86   Parrington had played football . . . a student at Harvard: Clark, p. 253.

86   took away from his experience . . . dominated the line of scrimmage.: Clark, p. 30.

86   because it interfered with a heavy teaching load,: Clark, p. 35.

86   The scholarly Parrington laid . . . football which were to come.: Clark, p. 35.

87   the school president failed . . . call OU officials to apologize.: Clark, p. 148.

87   "was a positive indicator": Clark, p. 146.

87   On April 27, 1967, as he headed . . . about 1 a.m. with the news.: Clark, p. 147.

87   he rushed to the hospital. . . . More than six hundred people: Clark, pp. 147-48.

87   I'll never forget, that was the last statement Jim Mackenzie made to me.: Clark, p. 147.

88   State led by seven points . . . with an offensive rebound.: Justin Harper, "Neal Delivers for OU," *The Oklahoman*, Feb. 19, 2006, p. 1C.

88   The winning field goal this . . . the last Texas Tech game.: John Rohde, "Nothing Comes Easy on the Road," *The Oklahoman*, Feb. 21, 2006, p. 1B.

88   The lead changed hands three . . . charity shots for the win.: Justin Harper, "Frantic Finish," *The Oklahoman*, Feb. 28, 2006, p. 1C.

89   if they needed discipline, he would loan them some.: Snook, *"Then Bud Said to Barry*, p. 163.

89   "away-from-home father . . . loved him as our own father.": Snook, *"Then Bud Said to Barry*, p. 154.

89   For an OU football player, . . . preceded the punishment.: Snook, *"Then Bud Said to Barry*, p. 156.

89   He was credited with saving . . . rarely spoke of the war.: Snook, *"Then Bud Said to Barry*, p. 152.

89   Wade Walker, an All-American . . . live up to that promise.": Snook, *"Then Bud Said to Barry*, p. 156.

89   I never recall him . . . anything out of character.: Snook, *"Then Bud Said to Barry*, p. 161.

90   Lewis Baker grew up in a . . . I see it now.": Jake Trotter, "Brotherly Love," *The Oklahoman*, Oct. 11, 2007, p. 1C.

90   Now I see Joe was just . . . appreciate him for that.: Trotter, "Brotherly Love."

91   Information about the 1951 College World Series and the OU champions comes from "Baseball: NCAA Tournament History: 1951 National Champions,"*SoonerSports.com*, http://www.soonersports.com/sports/m-basebl/archive/51-national-champs.html.

91   "despicable, vile, unprincipled scoundrels.": .": John MacArthur, *Twelve Ordinary Men* (Nashville: W Publishing Group, 2002), p. 152.

91   They weren't supposed to . . . even supposed to be that good.: "Baseball: NCAA Tournament History: 1951 National Champions."

92   His family arrived in Texas . . . to be recognized back there,": Simon Clancy, "Oklahoma Linebacker Tom Wort a Stranger in His Homeland," *Sports Illustrated*, March 23, 2011, http://sportsillustrated.cnn.com/2011/football/ncaa/03/23/tom-wort-oklahoma/index.html.

92   Until Wort, perhaps its most . . . at the 1972 Olympics.: Clancy, "Oklahoma Linebacker Tom Wort."

92   An informal survey at the . . . would be amazing.": Clancy, "Oklahoma Linebacker Tom Wort."

92   It's frustrating to be . . . I'm doing at OU.: Clancy, "Oklahoma Linebacker Tom Wort."

93   K-State's plan was obvious: . . . forgot No. 14 was back there.": George Schroeder, "Heupel's Air Attack Conquers No. 2 K-State," *No 1 Better* (Oklahoma City: *The Oklahoman*, 2001), p. 44.

93	"Now I think the country . . . "We're No. 1.'": Schroeder, "Heupel's Air Attack," p. 44.
93	Welcome back.: Schroeder, "Heupel's Air Attack," p. 44.
94	The word had already spread across the country: the King was dead.: Jim Dent, "Sooner Magic Never Failed Switzer's Teams," ESPN.com, Nov. 19, 2003, http://espn.go.com/ classic/s/2001/1024/1268485.html.
94	"was upon its deathbed.": Dent, "Sooner Magic."
94	The team gathered in the tiny . . . from a naked light bulb.": Dent, "Sooner Magic."
94	He told his team to forget . . . could do by three touchdowns.: Keith, p. 207.
94	"Gentlemen, there is only one . . . That person is me.": Dent, "Sooner Magic."
94	Then he left again. . . . go out and get it done.": Keith, p. 207.
94	The players "practically knocked . . . still ringing in their ears,: Dent, "Sooner Magic."
95	"We just knew we could . . . "It was a burden at times.": Snook, What It Means to Be a Sooner, p. 129.
95	Owens had carried the . . . "you imagine that today?": Snook, What It Means to Be a Sooner, p. 129.
95	He ran a sweep for his . . . done carrying the ball yet.": Snook, What It Means to Be a Sooner, p. 129.
95	Owens ran the ball six straight times after the time out: Snook, What It Means to Be a Sooner, p. 129.
95	Easy. Coach Switzer makes . . . a day during practice.: Snook, What It Means to Be a Sooner, p. 129.
96	From 1915-1928, Mex . . . accessible to non-ticketholders.": "Athletics: Oklahoma Tradition: Mex the Dog," SoonerSports.com, http://www.soonersports.com/trads/schooner-mascots.html.
96	Mex would often clear the field . . . ran a play nearby.: Upchurch, pp. 10-11.
96	Homeless and abandoned, . . . casket under Memorial Stadium.: "Athletics: Oklahoma Tradition."
97	The youngest of eight children, . . . there for the family games.: Susie Magill, "Center of Attention." Sharing the Victory, March 2009, http://www.sharingthevictory.com/vsItemDisplay.1sp? method=display&objectid=09AC87.
97	"I was a 20-20-20 man . . . or with 20 seconds left.": Kelli Anderson, "Double-Double Trouble," Sports Illustrated, Feb. 6, 2006, http://sportsillustrated.cnn.com/vault/article/magazine/ MAG1105926/index.htm.
97	"He was awful at it,": Magill, "Center of Attention."
97	Paris Senior taught his children . . . a student, and a Christian.: Magill, "Center of Attention."
97	God has shown me so much . . . and work for Him.: Magill, "Center of Attention."
98	"I loved to play . . . imitate what they did.: Snook, What It Means to Be a Sooner, p. 261.
98	Oubre almost signed out . . . missed his appointment.: Snook, What It Means to Be a Sooner, p. 262.
98	While they watched a film . . . have gone to Oklahoma.": Snook, What It Means to Be a Sooner, p. 263.
98	head coach Barry Switzer . . . it off with Oubre's mama.: Snook, What It Means to Be a Sooner, p. 263.
98	One night about 10, . . . she hung up on him.: Snook, What It Means to Be a Sooner, p. 262.
98	My mom [was] running . . . it came to recruiting.: Snook, What It Means to Be a Sooner, p. 262.
99	he "helped America win . . . build a football dynasty.": Berry Tramel, "Oklahoma Football: Former Sooner Merle Dinkins Dies at 87," NewsOK.com, Feb. 13, 2012, http://newsok.com/oklahoma-football.
99	before the Gator Bowl of . . . a watch or $125 cash.: Keith, pp. 7-8.
99	The players voted for the money. . . . pair of silk underwear.: Keith, p. 8.
99	That's the only time in . . . seven-dollar silk underpants.: Keith, p. 8.
100	Bob Stoops' assertion that his . . . made with his elbows.: John Rohde, "Chester Is a Triple Threat," The Oklahoman, Oct. 24, 2007, p. 1B.
100	In the spring of 2005, . . . was an excellent blocker,: Rohde, "Chester Is a Triple Threat."
100	offensive line coach Kevin Wilson . . . the team needed his help,: Jeff Huffman and Ed Thompson, "Getting to Know: Oklahoma OL Chris Chester," Coltpower.com, March 17, 2006, http://ind. scout.com/2/509896.html.

BIBLIOGRAPHY

Anderson, Bobby. "Boomer Bio: Patty Gasso." Sooner Spectator Magazine. 16 Feb. 2006. http://www.soonerspectator. com/featureStory.php?id=97.

Anderson, Kelli. "Back from the Dead." Sports Illustrated. 18 March 2002. http://sportsillustrated.cnn.com/vault/ article/magazine/MAG1025163/index.htm.

---. "Double-Double Trouble." Sports Illustrated. 6 Feb. 2006. http://sportsillustrated.cnn.com/vault/article/magazine/ MAG1105926/index.htm.

---. "Post Impressionist." Sports Illustrated. 26 Jan. 2009. http://sportsillustrated.cnn.com/vault/article/magazine/ MAG1150929/index.htm.

---. "Price is Right." Sports Illustrated. 21 Jan. 2002. http://sportsillustrated.cnn.com/vault/article/magazine/ MAG1024800/index.htm.

"Athletics: Oklahoma Tradition: Mex the Dog." *SoonerSports.com*. http://www.soonersports.com/trads/schooner-mascots.html.

"Athletics: Patty Gasso." *SoonerSports.com*. http://www.soonersports.com/school-bio/patty_gasso.html.

Baldwin, Mike. "Patience Pays Off for DE Macon." *The Oklahoman*. 14 Oct. 2010. 1C, 4C.

"Baseball: NCAA Tournament History: 1951 National Champions." *SoonerSports.com*. www.soonersports.com/sports/m-basebl/archive/51-national-champs.html.

"Baseball: NCAA Tournament History: 1994 National Champions." *SoonerSports.com*. www.soonersports.com/sports/m-basebl/archive/94-national-champs.html.

"Billy Vessels (1931-2001)." *Encyclopedia of Oklahoma History & Culture*. http://digital.library.okstate.edu/encyclopedia/entries/V/VE005.html.

Carlson, Jenni. "Driver Recalls the Schooner Slipup." *The Oklahoman*. 8 Sept. 2006. 1A.

---. "Giant Leaps; No Bounds for OU Gymnast." *The Oklahoman*. 2 March 2010. http://newsok.com/jenni-carlson-giant-leaps-no-bounds-for-ou-gymnast/article/3443170.

---. "Love Was in the Air for Stewart." *The Oklahoman*. 30 May 2000. http://newsok.com/article/2699282.

---. "Oklahoma's Frank Alexander: A Son on the Rise Playing for a Father on the Mend." *The Oklahoman*. 12 Oct. 2011. 1C.

---. "Sherri Coale Sets Tough Mindset for Sooners." *The Oklahoman*. 19 March 2012. http://news.ok.com/ou-womens-basketball.

Chen, Albert. "A Punishing Run." *Sports Illustrated*. 15 Dec. 2008. http://sportsillustrated.cnn.com/vault/article/magazine/MAG1149625/index.htm.

Clancy, Simon. "Oklahoma Linebacker Tom Wort a Stranger in His Homeland." *Sports Illustrated*. 23 March 2011. http://sportsillustrated.cnn.com/2011/football/ncaa/03/23/tom-wort-oklahoma/index.html.

Clark, J. Brent. *Sooner Century: 100 Glorious Years of Oklahoma Football*. Coal Valley, IL: Quality Sports Publications, 1995.

Cooley, Joshua. "Saving the Sooners." *Sharing the Victory*. http://www.sharingthevictory.com/vsItemDisplay.lsp?method=display&objectid=7C71871.

Culpepper, R. Alan. "The Gospel of Luke: Introduction, Commentary, and Reflections." *The New Interpreter's Bible*. Vol. IX. Nashville: Abingdon Press, 1998. 1-490.

Dent, Jim. "Sooner Magic Never Failed Switzer's Teams." *ESPN.com*. 19 Nov. 2003. http://espn.go.com/classic/s/2001/1024/1268485.html.

Dunn, Nick. "Above All Else." *FCA.org*. 16 March 2009. http://www.fac.org/vsItemDisplay.lsp&objectID=4CE3B38A.

Estel, Will. "Oklahoma Student Athlete Spotlight: Jelena Cerina." *Big12Sports.com*. 15 Feb. 2012. http://www.big12sports.com/ViewArticle.dbml?DB_OEM_ID=10410&ATCLID=205379.

Evans, Thayer. "Broyles' Playbook Now the Good Book." *FoxSports.com*. 17 Sept. 2011. http://msn.foxports.com/collegefootball/story.

"Football: All-American: Forest 'Spot' Geyer." *SoonerSports.com*. http://www.soonersports.com/sports/m-footbl/archive/aa-forest-geyer-1915.html.

"Football: Head Coaches: Barry Switzer (1973-1988)." *SoonerSports.com*. http://www.soonersports.com/sports/m-footbl/archive/head_coaches.html.

Forde, Pat. "Landry Jones' Maturity on Full Display." *ESPN.com*. 17 Sept. 2011. http://espn.go.com/college-football/story/_/id/6988141.

Gillman, Andrew. "OU's Hazewinkel Vows to Work at NCAAs." *The Oklahoman*. 16 March 2005. 1C.

Hack, Damon. "A Shoulder to Lean On." *Sports Illustrated*. 26 April 2010. http://sportsillustrated.cnn.com/vault/article/magazine/MAG1168636/index.htm.

Harper, Justin. "Frantic Finish: Sooners Make Cowboys Fourth Straight One-Point Victim." *The Oklahoman*. 28 Feb. 2006. 1C.

---. "Neal Delivers for OU." *The Oklahoman*. 19 Feb. 2006. 1C.

Helsley, John. "Rocha Worked His Way Back into Sooner Rotation." *The Oklahoman*. 19 May 2011. 5C.

---. "Sooners Catch Fire, Beat OSU." *The Oklahoman*. 5 Feb. 2007. 2OB.

Herndon, Booton. "Bud Wilkinson: The Winningest Coach in Football." Mark Stallard, ed. *Echoes of Oklahoma Sooners Football: The Greatest Stories Ever Told*. Chicago: Triumph Books, 2007. 147-63.

Hersch, Hank. "King Reigns." *Sports Illustrated*. 25 Nov. 1992. http://sportsillustrated.cnn.com/vault/article/magazine/MAG1142563/index.htm.

Hersom, Bob. "Resler Is Inspiring Force on OU Line." *The Oklahoman*. http://newsok.com/article/2369386.

Hoffer, Richard. "Big Man on Campus." *Sports Illustrated*. 28 Sept. 1992. http://sportsillustrated.cnn.com/vault/article/magazine/MAG1004272/index.htm.

Huffman, Jess and Ed Thompson. "Getting to Know: Oklahoma OL Chris Chester." *Coltpower.com*. 17 March 2006. http://ind.scout.com/2/509896.html.

"J.C. Watts." *Wikipedia, the free encyclopedia*. http://en.wikipedia.org/wiki/J._C._Watts.

Johnson, Roy S. "Oklahoma Rallies and Earns Berth in Orange Bowl." Mark Stallard, ed. *Echoes of Oklahoma Sooners Football: The Greatest Stories Ever Told*. Chicago: Triumph Books, 2007. 31-32.

Keith, Harold. *Forty-Seven Straight: The Wilkinson Era at Oklahoma*. Norman: University of Oklahoma Press, 2003.

MacArthur, John. *Twelve Ordinary Men*. Nashville: W Publishing Group, 2002.

Magill, Susie. "Center of Attention." *Sharing the Victory*. March 2009. http://www.sharingthe

victory.com/vsItemDisplay.1sp?method=display&objectid=09AC87.
---. "'Coales' of Wisdom." *Sharing the Victory.* March 2009. http://www.sharingthevictory.com/vsItemDisplay.1sp?
    method=display&objectid=09AC87.
Murphy, Austin. "Boomer Sooner." *Sports Illustrated.* 15 Oct. 2001. http://sportsillustrated.cnn.com/vault/article/
    magazine/MAG1023973/index.htm.
---. "Sooner Boomers." Mark Stallard, ed. *Echoes of Oklahoma Sooners Football: The Greatest Stories Ever Told.* Chicago:
    Triumph Books, 2007. 33-37.
---. "Take That, Texas!" *Sports Illustrated.* 1 Dec. 2008. http://sportsillustrated.cnn.com/vault/article/magazine/
    MAG1149149/index.html.
---. "The Oklahoma Kid." *Sports Illustrated.* 11 Oct. 2004. http://sportsillustrated.cnn.com/vault/article/magazine/
    MAG1105800/index.html.
Neri, G. "Wahoo! The Incredible Adventures of Chief Wahoo McDaniel: Wrestling Superstar." *HungerMountain.org.*
    31 July 2009. http://www.hungrymtn.org/wahoo.
"OU Golf Spotlight: Walter Emery." *SoonerSports.com.* 14 Sept. 2009. http://www.soonersports.com/spors/m-golf/
    spec-rel/091409aaa.html.
Palmer, Mark. "Christian Faith Serves Wrestlers On and Off the Mat." *Intermat.* 14 Aug. 2009. http://www.intermat
    wrestle.com/articles/5357.
Pond, David. "Sooner or Later." *Sharing the Victory.* Dec. 2009. http://www.sharingthevictory.com/vsItemDisplay.1sp
    ?method=display&objectid=4356375.
Putignano, Paul. "The Emotions of Sports: From a Low to a High." *the-signal.com.* 6 Aug. 2011. http://www.the-
    signal.com/archies/49133.
The Road to No. 1. Chicago: Triumph Books, 2003.
Rogers, Logan. "I'll Make Uwe Famous: 'The Kick' Could Be Called 'The Hold.'" *BleacherReport.com.* 4 Nov. 2009.
    http://bleacherreport.com/articles/283868.
Rohde, John. "Chester Is a Triple Threat." *The Oklahoman.* 14 Oct. 2007. 1B.
---. "Nothing Comes Easy on the Road." *The Oklahoman.* 21 Feb. 2006. 1B.
Schaller, Bob. *Faith of the Sooners: Inspiring Oklahoma Sports Stories of Faith.* Grand Island, NE: Cross Training
    Publishing, 2002.
Schroeder, George. "Back from the Brink." *The Oklahoman.* 12 March 2004. 1C.
---. "Big Crowd Gives OU Lift." *The Oklahoman.* 5 Feb. 2007. 20B.
---. "Classic: Sooners Outlast Cowboys in Epic Bedlam." *The Oklahoman.* 31 Oct. 2004. 1C.
---. "Griffin Scores 6 TD's Against UT." *No 1 Better.* Oklahoma City: *The Oklahoman,* 2001. 38, 40.
---. "Heupel's Air Attack Conquers No. 2 K-State." *No 1 Better.* Oklahoma City: *The Oklahoman,* 2001. 44, 47.
---. "Heupel's Dream in August Became Reality in January." *No 1 Better.* Oklahoma City: *The Oklahoman,* 2001.
    104-106.
---. "Hollis Price: Heartfelt Desire." *The Oklahoman.* 31 Aug. 2005. http://newsok.com/hollis-price-heartfelt-desire/
    article/1598301.
---. "OU's Bradley Hits His Stride.' *The Oklahoman.* 5 Nov. 2004. 5C.
---. "Sooners Conquer No. 1 Nebraska." *No 1 Better.* Oklahoma City: *The Oklahoman,* 2001. 50-53.
Schroeder, George & Berry Tramel. "A Season to Shout About." *No 1 Better.* Oklahoma City: *The Oklahoman,* 2001.
    6-11.
Shropshire, Mike. "Wahoo McDaniel." *Sports Illustrated.* 2 July 2001. http://sportsillustrated.cnn.com/vault/article/
    magazine/MAG1022918/index.htm.
Snook, Jeff. *"Then Bud Said to Barry Who Told Bob . . .".* Chicago: Triumph Books, 2008.
---. *What It Means to Be a Sooner.* Chicago: Triumph Books, 2005.
Strickland, Carter. "Just a Little Something to Believe In." *The Oklahoman.* 15 Oct. 2004. 1C.
Tramel, Berry. "Daryl Hunt: An OU Football Star of Substance." *Berry Tramel's Blog.* 14 July 2010. http://blog.newsok.
    com/berrytramel/2010/07/14.
---. "Oklahoma Football: Former Sooner Merle Dinkins Dies at 87." *NewsOKcom.* 13 Feb. 2012. http://newsok.com/
    oklahoma-football.
---. "Switzer Tales: Washington's Silver Shoes, Lott's Bandana." *Berry Tramel's Blog.* 13 May 2010. http://blog.newsok.
    com/berrytramel/2010/05/13.
---. "The Gospel of Sampson: Pride, Toughness Save OU." *The Oklahoman.* 12 March 2004. 13C.
---. "Young a War Hero, Kind Man." *The Oklahoman.* 30 Aug. 2007. http://newsok.com/young-a-war-hero.
Trotter, Jake. "10 Seasons Ago, 'Superman' Took Flight." *ESPN.com.* 6 Oct. 2011. http://espn.go.com/
    colleges/oklahoma/football/story/_/id/7065608.
---. "Back Where He Belongs." *The Oklahoman.* 12 Oct. 2010. 3C.
---. "Brotherly Love." *The Oklahoman.* 11 Oct. 2007. 1C.
---. "Decision to Stick It Out Paying Off for Oklahoma's Pryce Macon." *The Oklahoman.* 27 Dec. 2010. http://newsok.
    com/decision-to-stick-it-out.
Underwood, John. "Oklahomans Call It Selmonizing." *Sports Illustrated.* 12 Nov. 1973. http://sportsillustrated.cnn.
    com/vault/article/magazine/MAG1087997/index.htm.
Upchurch, Jay C. *Tales from the Sooners Sideline.* Champaign, IL: Sports Publishing L.L.C., 2007.
"Waddy Young." *Wikipedia, the free encyclopedia.* http://en.wikipedia.org/wiki/Waddy_Young.
Wright, Scott. "No Doghouse for Sooners' Godbold." *The Oklahoman.* 17 Feb. 2008. 1B.
---. "OU Football: 18 Tackles, Touchdown; Lofton's Game 'Outstanding.'" *The Oklahoman.* 16 Oct. 2007. 1C.

212

SOONERS

INDEX
(LAST NAME, DEVOTION DAY NUMBER)

OKLAHOMA

Mildren, Jack 52, 95
Minter, Alan 92
Mitchell, Jack 10, 51
Moore, Derland 40
Morgosh, Ray 91
Mosley, Wendell 63
Murphy, Austin 2
Murphy, Floyd 91
Murray, DeMarco 15, 50, 55
Murray, Jim 31
Neal, Michael 88
Neysmith, Tony 58
Norman, Josh 78
Oubre, Louis 98
Owen, Bennie 26, 34, 57, 96
Owens, Steve 29, 52, 74, 82, 87, 95
Owens, Tinker 82
Paige, Satchel 65
Paris, Ashley 97
Paris, Bubba 97
Paris, Courtney 97
Parrington, V.L. 17, 86
Peacock, Elvis 23
Perry, Fred 1
Peterson, Adrian 25, 81
Pettibone, Jerry 48, 98
Phillips, Anthony 11
Price, Hollis 37
Pugsley, Charley 91
Rawlinson, Ken 8, 87
Reeds, Claude 34
Resler, Jeff 11
Reuber, Alan 53
Rhodes, Steve 4, 23, 35, 48
Richards, Bob 67

Riley, Andrea 28
Risinger, Bud 1
Roberts, J.D. 77
Robertson, Port 89
Rocha, Michael 64
Royal, Darrell 19, 21, 80, 83
Ruster, Dan 19
Sampson, Kelvin 49
Sandefer, Jakie 71
Sandusky, John 8
Savage, Antwone 78
Selmon, Dewey 31, 69
Selmon, Lee Roy 31, 69
Selmon, Lucious 31, 69
Shelby, Brandon 18
Shepard, Derrick 22, 80
Shepard, Woodie 23
Shirley, Jack 91
Shults, Jessica 45
Sims, Billy 19, 25
Steffen, Roger 27
Steinbeck, John 39
Stewart, Jennifer 84
Stills, Kenny 9
Stoops, Bob 2, 5, 9, 27, 33, 38, 42, 50, 53, 73, 78, 85, 100
Stoops, Carol 2
Stoops, Mike 47, 85
Strickland, Carter 18
Stubblefield, Taylor 42
Switzer, Barry 4, 19, 22, 23, 31, 35, 39, 40, 43, 46, 52, 69, 80, 87, 95, 98
Tatum, Jim 8, 10, 39, 62, 99
Taylor, Adrian 73
Thatcher, J.T. 93

Thomas, Clendon 8
Thomas, George 83
Thompson, Michael 85
Tillman, Spencer 80
Tisdale, Wayman 7
Tramel, Berry 76
Trevino, Lee 23
Truman, Harry 10
Tubbs, Jerry 6, 94
Turner, Larry 49
Upchurch, Jay 31
Valora, Forrest 35
Venables, Brent 15, 33, 73
Vessels, Billy 56
von Schamann, Uwe 4
Waldrip, Jim 91
Walker, Barth 36
Walker, Wade 83, 89
Wantland, Charley 57
Washington, Joe 19, 43
Watts, J.C. 35
West, Stan 83
Whaley, Dominique 9
White, Jason 5, 18, 53, 61, 81, 85
Wilkinson, Bud 6, 8, 14, 39, 56, 60, 61, 62, 71, 77, 83, 94, 99
Williams, Roy 47
Wilson, Kevin 85, 100
Wilson-Guest, Jeremy 27, 78
Wort, Tom 92
Wright, Bobby Jack 73
Wuerffel, Danny 62
Wyatt, Darrell 81
Young, Roland 66
Zabel, Steve 87

214